Speaking of Writing

Conversations with Canadian Novelists

Ann Clayton

Clayton, Ann
    Speaking of Writing: Conversations with Canadian Novelists / Ann Clayton

Interviews.

ISBN: 978-1-928171-59-1 (pbk)
ISBN: 978-1-928171-60-7 (ebk)

Copyright © Ann Clayton, 2017

Cover image by Greg Denton / "Ann Clayton. 020/100, 100 Portraits/100 Poppies, 2015"

Vocamus Community Publications

130 Dublin Street North
Guelph, Ontario
N1H 4N4

Contents

Acknowledgements	iv
Preface	1
Canada Under Eastern Skies: Janice Kulyk Keefer	7
There Will Be Gardens: Alice Boissonneau	30
"Kawaiso" and Japanese-Canadians: Joy Kogawa	44
Restless Western Women: Aritha van Herk	63
When Words Deny the World: Stephen Henighan	88
The Irish Descendants: Jane Urquhart	107
Subverting Canadian Suburbia: Barbara Gowdy	135
Postscript	158

Acknowledgements

A version of "Interview with Janice Kulyk Keefer" first appeared as "Janice Kulyk Keefer Interviewed by Cherry Clayton" in *Journal of Commonwealth Literature* 34:2 (April 1999): 183-197.

A version of "Interview with Alice Boissonneau" first appeared as "Pressed Between the Pages of Balzac: Cherry Clayton Speaks with Alice Boissonneau" in *Books in Canada* (September 1999): 19-21.

A version of "Interview with Joy Kogawa" first appeared in *Canadian Ethnic Studies* 34:3 (2003): 106-116.

Preface

The interviews presented here all engage with the process by which writers revise and contest the boundaries of nation, state, and the more subjective lines of gender, family and literary traditions. The writers interviewed reflect on patterns of migrant labour, internal displacement and diasporas, and on the politics of narration in relation to specific regions, and to gender constructs.

The interview project began with women writers living in and around Guelph, set out in the spirit of a dialogue between an ex-South African writer and Canadian novelists in order to explore some of the complex weave created by different immigrant histories in Canada. The idea was to explore women writers' own sense of the development of their creativity and their place in any conception of Canadian traditions, both political and literary.

Canada has a dual heritage of British and French imperialism, and this dual heritage is in turn refracted through the multiple immigrant histories of later arrivals, and the regional autonomy which contest any centralized state power in Canada. This complexity is seen at work in Janice Kulyk Keefer's representations of Acadian culture in the Maritimes, French cultural neo-imperialism, and language codes in eastern Canada. It is also evident in Jane Urquhart's revisioning of the power of Louis XIV in her poetry volume, *The Little Flowers of Madame de Montespan*, in Aritha van Herk's feminist challenges to genre codes in western Canada, and Joy Kogawa's narratives of Japanese-Canadian post-war displacement from British Columbia.

Alice Boissonneau's fictions and memoirs work with a Toronto economic underclass in post-war Canada, and show an earlier cycle of labour displacement from Ireland to Canada, and from small Ontario towns to Toronto. Her fiction relates problems of women schooled to forms of dependence, the wartime conscription or displacement of men, and the spiritual process by which inner freedom is achieved. In this respect her work parallels with Kogawa's narratives, in which psychological emancipation is closely tied to the effects of war and economic depression on family structures, young women's lives, the curtailment of possibilities, and a moral radiance which springs from suffering understood and worked through in time and storytelling.

Canada has had close ties with England, Ireland and Scotland, and there are strong forms of continuity with European literary traditions, even though writers also rework those traditions to illuminate both Canadian cultural dependence and relative autonomy. The picaresque novel is refashioned by van Herk in *No Fixed Address*, and the male, imperial narrative of polar expeditions in *The Tent Peg* and *Places Far from Ellesmere*. British Romantic poetry and fiction are a strong presence in Jane Urquhart's work, and some of the key figures of Romantic literature walk through her pages and have speaking roles. Van Herk is concerned to give Tolstoy's *Anna Karenina* a different plot and ending. Kulyk Keefer writes back to Virginia Woolf and Katherine Mansfield in a form of sequential postmodernism in her earlier stories and in *Rest Harrow*. The figure of the Canadian female researcher who travels to England and makes unexpected discoveries about herself and her own belonging is found in Kulyk Keefer and Urquhart's novels.

Joy Kogawa's fiction is allied to the minimalist genres of Oriental art in the lyrical delicacy of *Obasan*, and she draws on this formal legacy, as well as the closely knit families of Japanese-Canadian culture, to question the violence of neo-imperialism and the Cold War, and the treatment of minorities in Canada. Wartime experience, and atomic bombings, become an extreme case of the more widespread economic marginalization of minority groups within liberal democracies.

Barbara Gowdy's fiction defamiliarizes suburbia and the family to show how unstable gender categories and conservative family mores actually are in everyday life. She draws on American traditions of the grotesque, absurd and extreme humour to illuminate the extremities of alienation found in a world of capitalist consumerism, media domination, and the legacy of the fifties suburban North American dream. The reduced emotional lives of Western capitalism are figured in bizarre physicality, disasters, and deformities. Her construction of a matriarchal African elephant kingdom has profound resonance in a world that now struggles with ecological problems, but her elephants also tell us a great deal about the kinds of connection human beings need in order to thrive.

In the interviews gathered here, I sought to create an open forum in dialogue with writers who actually live in the Guelph area or nearby, or were visiting Guelph for conferences, guest lectures or honorary doctorates. The interviews rely on the generosity and candour of the writers, their self-insights and retrospective understanding, at this point, of their own literary production and its relation to the broader Canadian scene. The interviews were most enjoyable and instructive for me, as a relatively new Canadian.

In particular, I attempted to highlight in discussion some of the comparative grounds between South African and Canadian history, politics and culture. With South Africa's late democratization, in 1994, and Canada's involvement in the election process, trade unions, and other professional and industrial activities, substantial grounds exist for comparative analysis. The Oka crisis and First Nations land claims in recent Canadian history make struggles for postcolonial restitution, and the clearer recognition of cultural damage, shared terrain in South Africa and Canada, as the Kogawa interview demonstrates. In Canada, as in South Africa, a fuller recognition of ethnicity, of the orality of indigenous traditions, and diversity within gender constructs, followed after the wave of cultural nationalism that put national literatures on a university curriculum previously heavily weighted towards British literature.

The interviews also illuminate some of the conditions of women writers in exile or living with a sense of difference from the dominant culture, sometimes as minorities with a minority language and heritage in Canada, or as immigrant descendants reworking their ethnic heritages in a process of cultural adaptation. Even Ontario writers often narrate small town or suburban Canadian life so as to make it deeply unrecognizable and yet sanely familiar (Boissonneau, Urquhart and Gowdy). The particular regional tensions of western Canada and of the Maritimes, as against a posited Toronto "centre", are revealed in the van Herk and Kulyk Keefer interviews. The interview dialogues are part of a dynamic mosaic illustrating tradition and talent, forms of solidarity and difference, the difficulty of the writing process and critical reception, and the multiple conversations individuals and communities hold with one another across borders and oceans.

What women writers have in common is a heightened sense of marginality, a sense of speaking back to women forebears, and a conscious manipulation of genre codes that are perceived as implicit in a social order previously inimical to women as writers and citizens. At the same time, women writers have many bonds with national and international communities, and feminism is by no means a conscious agenda with all the writers interviewed here. The particular tensions between conscious aims and unconscious processes, biography and literature, early and later work in a still evolving process, are the striking features of interviews between writers from different national arenas, and may be useful in scholarship and critical reevaluation.

I should like to thank the writers who consented to be interviewed and who offered their time, insights, intellectual stimulus, and difficult self-understandings so generously. Many thanks to Stephen Henighan of the University of Guelph for adding his understanding of gender codes, Canada, and Europe, and for commenting on his own life and writing, especially in relation to Latin America. I should also like to thank the Canada Council for a grant which helped with the dissemination of some aspects of the Canadian interviewing project at conferences in Europe, and James Walster for making the videotapes of interviews from which these transcripts were made. The University of Guelph offered many forms of technical assistance for interviews as well as other resources, forms of training, and stimulating students who have given me many insights into Canadian cultural life. Cathy Voight assisted with publicity arrangements when visiting writers were in town. Tim Struthers kindly arranged for me to interview Joy Kogawa at a conference he organized at The University of Guelph in November 1999, "A Visionary Tradition: Canadian Literature at the Turn of the Millennium". Alice Boissonneau has been unfailingly helpful with resources regarding Canadian writers and their organizations.

I hope these interviews contribute to a comparative discussion of culture, politics and society in South Africa and Canada, and illuminate some of the complex processes by which writers narrate other lives in order to comprehend their own.

Ann Clayton, Guelph, Ontario

Canada Under Eastern Skies: Janice Kulyk Keefer

Janice Kulyk Keefer was born in Toronto, Ontario in 1952, is of Ukrainian and Polish descent, and was educated in Canada and England. She has taught literature and creative writing in France and Nova Scotia, and at the University of Guelph, Ontario.

She has published three volumes of poetry: *White of the Lesser Angels* (1986), *Marrying the Sea* (1998), and *Midnight Stroll* (2006); several volumes of criticism: *Under Eastern Eyes: A Critical Reading of Maritime Fiction* (1987), *Reading Mavis Gallant.* New York: Oxford UP, (1989).

Precarious Present/Promising Future?: Ethnicities and Identities in Canadian Literature. (co-edited with Richard E. Sherwin and Danielle Schaub, 1996), *Two Lands, New Visions: Stories from Canada and Ukraine* (co-edited with Solomea Pavlychk, 1998), and *Dark Ghost in the Corner: Imagining Ukrainian-Canadian Identity* (2005); and a memoir: *Honey and Ashes: A Story of Family* (1998). Kulyk Keefer's fiction includes *The Paris-Napoli Express* (1986), *Transfigurations* (1987), *Constellations* (1988), *Travelling Ladies* (1990), *Rest Harrow* (1992), *The Green Library* (1996), *Anna's Goat* (2000) and *Thieves.* (2004).

Under Eastern Eyes was nominated for the 1987 Governor General's Award, *Constellations* was nominated for the 1988 Books in Canada First Novel Award, and *The Green Library* was nominated for the 1996 Governor General's Awards. Kulyk Keefer was also awarded the 1999 Marian Engel Award for an outstanding body of prose works by a Canadian woman writer.

Kulyk Keefer's fiction works with histories of dispossession in Acadian, indigenous (Micmac) and Ukrainian communities within

Canada. She speaks of cultivating a "transcultural ethic", one which challenges the dominant critical and cultural paradigms of Northrop Frye and Margaret Atwood. Her writing decentralizes Canadian literary paradigms in terms of region, expatriate communities and diasporic cultures. Her own critical work has examined the achievements of major novelists who were both nationally displaced and yet central to the European literary canon: Joseph Conrad and Henry James. In Canada her critical attention has been given to a Canadian writer who chose to live in Paris, Mavis Gallant; to the marginal voices of the Eastern seaboard and its communities, especially the women writers of Nova Scotia; and to multicultural identities.

Kulyk Keefer's version of postmodern art lies in her multiple, heterogenous narratives, which draw on overlapping perspectives and dream landscapes. Her fictional strategies include the use of photography and newsprint to evoke the relationship between media and art, and our shifting identities in a globalized consumer culture. She draws on travel metaphors, like Albertan novelist, Aritha van Herk, to evoke both the indeterminacy of contemporary life and a continuing quest for a stable framework within family, memory, and literary reconstruction. Her characters include women researchers to the United Kingdom, French neo-imperialists in Canada, and Canadian descendants of Ukrainian immigrants journeying to Eastern Europe.

Kulyk Keefer's vision is a contemporary Canadian one, evoking not settler myths of survival in a hostile environment but daily existence in a complex urban globalized culture. Immigrant histories contend with assimilation, as in daily Canadian life. By depicting the localized history of the Maritimes and an imagined Ukrainian hinterland, Kulyk Keefer's work illustrates and breaks down barriers of class and culture.

Interview with Janice Kulyk Keefer

AC: In your critical study of Maritime fiction, *Under Eastern Eyes*, you contest a number of models of Canadian national literature. You mention Northrop Frye's models of a frontier society, and east-west models of exploration and development. Were you deliberately setting up alternative models of the nation and of literary history?

JKK: The Maritimes is a distinctive region, so I was seeing it as paradigmatic but not as prescriptive. Canada is a nation of diverse regions and it is foolish and reductive to generalize about 'the' Canadian literary tradition, 'the' Canadian response to nature, or 'the' Canadian experience of culture. Although there are not many people in this huge country, there are many diverse forms of cultural and social experience that have been mined by artists. Having grown up in Ontario and having lived out of the country for a number of years, when I returned to Canada via a region that I hadn't known at all, I felt myself a virtual newcomer after my years in England and France. I knew almost nothing about Maritime literature in general or in specifics. I even managed to escape reading Lucy Maud Montgomery when I was a kid, so I was totally ignorant of Maritime fiction except for *The Mountain and the Valley* and a few Charles G. D. Roberts stories, so I thought the best way to reacquaint myself with my country after an absence of about eight years was to study the literature of the region.

If I'd had any illusions that reading Maritime literature would give me a template for reading Canadian literature as a whole, those illusions were quickly dispelled by the incredible variety and specificity of the texts I was reading, and I did start with the very earliest texts, which are also the very earliest Canadian texts. It became clear to me that even though I hadn't studied very much Canadian literature when I was an undergraduate at the University of Toronto, there was a world of difference between Susanna Moodie's *Roughing It in the Bush* or *Life in the Clearing*s and the accounts of someone like Joseph Howe or Thomas McCullough or Haliburton's views of colonial not pioneer life, a kind of settled, "civilized" Nova Scotia, New Brunswick and Prince Edward Island. The texts were giving me very interesting, unexpected readings of a particular culture that did not seem to relate to what I knew of the so-called Canadian scene, the impressions I got from Northrop Frye and others.

AC: Have Margaret Atwood's ideas of sustaining central myths of survival and victimization in Canadian literature been significant for you, or myths you have reacted against?

JKK: By the time I was coming of intellectual age, Margaret Atwood's book, *Survival*, was being contested; it was no longer being received as the first and final word on the Canadian psyche and sensibility. *Survival* was a very interesting text, a provocative and polemical text designed to do a kind of magician's trick. It appeared to offer an instant critical position, but as soon as you began to compare the theses of *Survival* with the texts you'd read outside the central Canadian milieu, *Survival* showed its own inadequacies as any kind of master narrative for the whole nation.

AC: I noticed that in your critical work you want to decentralize, to show variety and diversity within the literary context.

JKK: That comes out of the lived experience of being and working in a region considered to be off the Canadian map. I can't tell you how many times I would turn on the CBC Radio in Church Point, Nova Scotia, and hear an account of Canada that ended in Montreal. I bridled when I read Northrop Frye's account of how the first settlers or explorers came to Canada: there was this foggy bit of the map, known as the Maritimes, but civilization began at Quebec and Montreal.

AC: Within *Under Eastern Eyes* you seemed to be tracing the emergence of a woman's voice, perhaps a postmodern voice, against an older, canonical tradition created by male writers.

JKK: I was also trying to contest the primacy of Charles G.D. Roberts as forefather. If we must have a Freudian family romance for Canadian culture, it seemed to me more important to talk about Lucy Maud Montgomery as the parent of Canadian literature in terms of Canada's profile on the international literary scene. Certainly people were reading Lucy Maud Montgomery all over the world, and in translation, long after they read Charles G.D. Roberts. There was this extraordinary refusal to concede not just the popularity, but also the abiding interest of Montgomery's work. Not just her fiction, but also the journals, which Mary Rubio and Elizabeth Waterston have done such a splendid job of editing. We now have a portrait of a writer and woman who was a contemporary of Virginia Woolf's, quite an extraordinary person who was struggling with colonialism, with being a woman in a man's world, and with being a regional writer who is displaced to the centre and finds all kinds of things falling apart when she is located at that centre. Her life is fascinating, and her work repays a lot of careful attention, particularly since our notions of culture have broadened to include the popular and non-canonical forms of literature.

AC: Do you think she's also been underrated because she's been classified as a writer for children?

JKK: Yes, and for girl children in particular. Alice Munro and Jane Urquhart have both talked about the importance of *Emily of New Moon* in their lives.

AC: I'd like to consider your first novel, *Constellations*, set in a small coastal village in the Maritimes, against the cultural history you outline in your critical book. The Acadian community you represent in that novel could be considered representative of subsistence struggle in many parts of Canada, and of cultural isolation and forms of dependence. They have a history of dispossession and exile, quite a romantic history. But at the time you write about it's settled into a fairly conservative format. Were you drawing on Jane Austen's recipe for the novel: take a few settled families in a small village and see how their interaction unfolds? There seemed to be a European novel form at work, but with specifically Canadian cultural interactions and resentments.

JKK: Yes, but I'd say that the Jane Austen model is the last one I had in mind, partly because Austen is so careful to delineate what she will write about, which families will form the circumference of the social world she is able to depict. I think it's in *Emma* that she says she will not consider "these kinds of people" outside a certain social sphere, rather like E.M. Forster, in *Howard's End*, saying, "About the poor we have nothing to say."

AC: The poor are always with us, but we won't write about them.

JKK: Austen is very upfront about that, I think, whereas the Spruce Harbour community I write about is already highly heterogenous. There are Acadians who are really newcomers there, who have been dispossessed from the very fertile Annapolis Valley, from Grand-Pré, down to the Atlantic seaboard. Later, there was a kind of resurgence. If you read someone like Antonine Maillet's *Pelagie* you see Acadians trickling back to Grand-Pré and finding their farms have been taken over, either by New Englanders or the British. So they are doubly dispossessed and have to start a new life in the very grudging soil of certain coastal areas of New Brunswick and Nova Scotia. The Acadian community in the Maritimes is itself heterogeneous. The Acadians in New Brunswick are more numerous than those of Nova Scotia and their cultural presence is much stronger. There are many more writers among them; Maillet is a New Brunswick Acadian. There is the interesting phenomenon of Acadians of mixed Micmac and French background, but there was a taboo against mentioning that background. The character Mariette in *Constellations* comes from the mixed heritage and is not able to acknowledge that mixture, because it's denied by the whole culture.

AC: Is her disappearance at the end of the novel related to that; she's an unacknowledged element in that society?

JKK: Everyone knows she's there, but people refuse to talk with or about her in ways that are at all helpful, that would give Mariette agency or a significant status. That contributes to marginality. Her gender is another issue. So is her socio-economic position, as important as her Acadian / Micmac background. I decided I didn't want to write a novel with a straight linear narrative and a fixed point of view, but wanted to jump around in the heads of many different characters including the *francais de France*, who is a complete stranger, and the principal character Claire, whose mother is English-from-England and whose father is Acadian, and who therefore doesn't belong anywhere, doesn't feel at home in Europe, in Spruce Harbour, doesn't feel Acadian, and certainly doesn't feel Canadian, unless one defines Canadian as being at home anywhere, as constantly being *a la rechereche de son pays*. I was always aware while I was writing that novel that I was living as a stranger in a community that felt itself to be a floating island, and whose cultural traditions were curiously imperial, with the whole tradition of Longfellow's poem *Evangeline* being used to define Acadian identity. *Evangeline* is a story of losers, where the story of expulsion becomes a version of the fortunate fall: they can all move down to Louisiana where the climate is so much better. So the whole thing is very layered.

AC: It reminded me in some ways of Olive Schreiner's *African Farm*, of isolated African communities where it becomes a major thing if you leave, you become an outsider, and then the question is will the person return, and will you be so changed you can no longer readapt. That told me something about cultural isolation in Spruce Harbour.

JKK: I did have the character Hector who goes off to Quebec to study philosophy and who returns to be a janitor philosopher. He resists the romanticizing of Acadian culture, and wants to find some kind of integrity in his Acadian identity, to review his botched relationships with people there, his failure to establish lasting connections. His failure to become the good Acadian boy his parents wanted is not so much an index to his total failure as a sense of his cultural identity being a constant struggle to react against the negative elements that are killing the culture under the guise of protecting it. I see him as a very positive character. Mariette has an obviously tragic trajectory in the novel. I had in mind a foil to the Bertrand character, the cultural imperialist interloper and impresario, and the artist manqué because he has no clue what art really involves.

AC: Is Halyna, the musician, another satirical version of the European artist, who wants to gain cultural prestige by going to Paris?

JKK: The important thing is that she's Eastern European, Polish, and comes from another colonized country. She has this combination of real artistry and practical performance, but she's also the arch-professional, and has the ruthlessness of someone who knows what she needs. I'm thinking of the young Katherine Mansfield setting off for London and saying: here's a little summary of what I need: wealth, power and freedom. That kind of ruthlessness is necessary, particularly for the woman artist.

AC: Was the ending of the novel, Claire's self-conflagration, meant as confirmation of a defensiveness within the Acadian community?

JKK: I was thinking of the ending of a novel like Conrad's *Victory*, which also has a fire and ends with a narrator coming in and observing the ruins of Axel Heyst's compound on a little island.

AC: Was it also a comment on her emotional isolation, her defences against affection for Hector?

JKK: Yes, but what Conrad has his character say is that sometimes an explosion is the most liberating thing in the world. Claire lives vicariously through other people. She's a kind of director, stage-producer, and she finds she can't do this with impunity, that her emotions come into play with a force that she hadn't reckoned with.

AC: And she comes up against the power of the institution, too, when she loses her job because of these personal involvements.

JKK: That notion of economic dependence, particularly as it touches the lives of women, was something I was very keen to bring to the fore in the novel, especially for women who choose not to marry, or who marry and live apart from their partners. I was also writing this in the context of a small, extremely conservative community, very traditional in its ways of being, and in relationships between the sexes.

AC: You've done a lot of work on the fiction of Mavis Gallant, have incorporated references to Katherine Mansfield, and your first collection of stories, *Travelling Ladies*, draws on themes of expatriation and displacement. Your wonderful story, "Paris-Napoli Express", about a Canadian travelling on the wrong train in Europe, recalls the pace and mood of a Mansfield story. Do you feel a special affinity for expatriate writers despite growing up entirely in Canada yourself? Does your own sense of marginality come from your experience of Ukrainian family history in Canada?

JKK: The question of marginality is tricky to talk about because of my ethnicity, which is Ukrainian and a bit of Polish, although I'm the daughter of first-generation immigrants. My skin colour doesn't give me away as "other", but the kind of childhood I had, the growing up between languages, the experiences my family had, of discrimination when coming to Canada, all filtered down and marked my sense of who I was. My sense of possibility, my sense of being Canadian, was not at all as powerfully inflected as it would have been had I been from the West Indies, for example, or Bombay, but there was enough sense of otherness to make me feel my ethnicity as a burden, in a sense, because we were always talking about "the English", never the Canadians, versus the "Nashi" or "our own". Part of me grew up thinking it was somehow my job to go and liberate my homeland.

AC: Even though "the English" were in fact often Scots?

JKK: That didn't count. Whether you were Irish or Scots – we didn't say Anglo-Celtic or even WASP, Just "the English".

AC: So it was a language distinction?

JKK: And a cultural distinction. On the one hand, I felt that difference was punitive, but I also felt there was a sense of privilege to being different from the boring English, and I was made to feel that we could compensate for our difference by being colourful and passionate.

AC: And you did benefit by your European heritage, the traditions and the stories?

JKK: Yes, but for Ukrainians one's identity has always been embattled and threatened, one's culture and language deformed by the imperial experience. Ukraine was largely a peasant culture until the nineteenth century, when a Ukrainian intelligentsia appeared even in Russified cities, such as Kyiv.

AC: Wouldn't the oral tradition of narrative have been important to you?

JKK: Yes, very strongly, and the family stories that I heard about my mother's life growing up in a small Polish village. When I decided that I wanted to get out of Canada, as an undergraduate, I'd always had this thing about "going back" to a place I'd never seen before. But on the way to Eastern Europe, I stopped off in Western Europe, and until 1997 I never went "home" to Ukraine. I studied in England and France, and when I came back to Canada, I spent a year in Ottawa, and I remember a crucial experience of walking into a department store there, and finding, remaindered on the table with winter gloves, a copy of Mavis Gallant's *From the Fourteenth District*. This was my very first real encounter with a living Canadian writer, apart from a survey course on CanLit at the University of Toronto.

AC: There's often a stronger loyalty after a return, I think. I know that motivated my work on novelist Olive Schreiner in South Africa.

JKK: Well, I opened this book, and there was a Canadian writer writing about European experience, abut the British, or Australians, or Americans in Europe. This was a revelation. You didn't have to write about Prairie wheatfields. The connection for me was extremely immediate because I'd just been living in Europe for eight years. I had all kinds of stories I'd written there. Do I throw them away because they're not Canadian, or do I redefine my notion of what Canadian identity means? And in some ways you never feel more Canadian than when you are living abroad, out of the country.

AC: And travelling on the wrong train?

JKK: Especially when you're on the wrong train, which of course never happens in this country.

AD: I've been known to get on wrong trains. I wanted to ask you about genres. You've described poems as "the eyes of stories". As I look at the way your literary oeuvre has changed, you seem to have moved from poetry to the novel.

JKK: I do have a new book of poetry out, *Marrying the Sea*.

AC: You've maintained a sense of being a poet as well?

JKK: Yes. We're also talking here about the kind of commercial milieu writers work in. Publishers don't really want to know if you've got a book of short stories or poetry. They want the novel, because novels can win Giller prizes and be made into movies. But then there's the poetic novel, such as Anne Michaels' *Fugitive Pieces*, which is a novel written like a poem. There are ways around the imperative of fiction, and of long narrative. It's not just what the publishers and reading public seem to demand; it's also a sense of the kind of freedom that the novel gives you, in terms of scope and invention. I still love reading and writing short fiction. The project I've been involved in since *The Green Library* is a family memoir, to be published this fall. This has taken me to yet another genre altogether – creative non-fiction.

AC: Well, hybridity is in.

JKK: Yes, but again, it has a lot to do with the whole notion of how we know ourselves through narrative, how we construct personal, family and national identities.

AC: In *The Green Library* you've incorporated social history, so that would also take you further into personal history. It seems a natural progression.

JKK: The first part of the new book, which is called *Honey and Ashes*, deals with the stories I grew up with, this timeless world of a small Polish village on the border between Poland and Soviet Ukraine. The middle part deals with the larger public world that surrounded and penetrated that timeless village, but which I never knew about until I grew up. So I have a section which is an attempt to contextualize family narrative. And then the third part is a travel narrative which takes me back physically to the village where my mother was born.

AC: You seem to have experimented with dream narratives and fantasies in which you investigate identity in a different way, and evoke a sense of threat or fragmentation. Are you wanting to do something different with identity in those poetic narratives? There are also poetic, fantasy sections within the novels.

JKK: I think poems and dreams come from the same place and are often what is most powerful in fiction. We need to bring logic and imagination together. I wouldn't want to say poetry is oneiric and fiction is the logical, waking self, and that the two must remain separate.

AC: Do you think poetry is a more therapeutic form of writing?

JKK: No, not at all. Dreams can often be terribly disturbing.

AC: And also tell us things about the real world.

JKK: "In dreams begin responsibilities," to quote Yeats. But I think what fascinates me about narrative in dreaming is the jumps, the leaps one makes. I think of a poet like John Thompson, or Phyllis Webb. When I'm teaching creative writing to students both in poetry and fiction, I tell them to think of how you dream, think of the narrative as a dream.

Ann Clayton

AC: In other words, chronology is not the key?

JKK: And it's not what Virginia Woolf called "beast of burden" work either, filling in details. This notion is of juxtaposition and what Freud called condensation, where things that in ordinary waking life would never appear connected or interdependent in dream-work are sewn up together. That's what can be so disconcerting but also so revealing.

AC: I know it can be really annoying when critics equate women with nationhood, but the heroine of your second novel, *Rest Harrow*, is called Anna English, and she does seem to go in pursuit of the English, who, as Doris Lessing tells us, are nowhere to be found. Is *Rest Harrow* about Canada's relationship with England and British cultural imperialism?

JKK: When I went to England I thought I was disburdening myself of a very problematic sense of Canadian identity, which for me was fraught by the way in which I'd grown up between cultures. I thought I could retrieve myself. I fell in love with everything English, with Virginia Woolf, with Woolf's Sussex, and London. I did my MA on Woolf, then got tired of Bloomsbury and did my doctoral work on Conrad and James, expatriate writers who still had the English connection, but were rather different in their allegiances and critical sense of their own countries.

I went back to Canada and found myself back in England ten years after I'd left it, on sabbatical, intending to write a rather Jane Austen-ish comedy of manners, set in a small English village. But we'd left the year that Thatcher was elected, and we came back on the tenth anniversary of that election, and it seemed that she would rule forever. I was with friends whose political, ontological situation had changed drastically. I also found myself living in a small Sussex village not far from Rodmell, and the time that I was supposed to spend writing my idyllic English novel, I spent devouring English newspapers in a way I'd never done in Canada: *The Guardian* and *The Independent*, and watching TV news. I was fascinated by the way in which TV news contains global narrative and by the sequence of narrative in the newspapers. I found the degree of political turmoil and despair in

England and worldwide amazing.

Because I was reading the papers, especially those with an international focus, I was suddenly aware of world events, in Asia and Iraq as well, and this crowded into my consciousness and thus the consciousness of the heroine I devised, who comes to England just to write her book on Woolf, and finds she can't do that. She's haunted by Woolf, but by a different Woolf than the creature she had constructed by reading the novels. It's the Woolf who is profoundly affected by the Depression and the war, by German bombers flying overhead.

AC: Yes, you made me think of the wartime context in the way you build up a sense of contemporary disaster in England, so that there's another suicide, and though it's not wartime, it could be, because the social context is so disastrous.

JKK: The fascinating thing is what happened after I wrote the novel – a novel in which one of the characters, Fiona, who seems a nice bland upper-middle class Englishwoman, turns out to be a woman whose husband has just left her and is quite devastated. She ends up taping photos and disaster stories to the walls of her study, so there's a newspaper wallpaper that brings that larger world into this small, privileged milieu. After I'd written the novel and started to teach contemporary British fiction and set Doris Lessing's *The Golden Notebook*, I found that Anna Wulf does the same thing. I thought that was interesting: there are literary foremothers that you write back to but haven't even read. I was intrigued by that, because there is a kind of continuing tradition, particularly for women.

AC: Who've been told they should have a conscience, and carry everyone's burden?

JKK: But also that conscience should pertain only to domestic private life, the personal sphere.

AC: I liked that Virginia Woolf ghost that kept flitting through your novel. It was a bit of a ghost story. She was there somewhere, but could never be located.

JKK: Although none of the reviewers picked up the references to Woolf texts, or could engage with the political subtext, which is perhaps understandable. I thought Thatcherism was such a worldwide phenomenon. Reagan was Thatcher in trousers, but the response made me recognize that this coding was not shared. I had references to Woolf, but also to Mandelstam and others.

AC: This was to broaden the political context?

JKK: Yes, and with the situation of writers who are sometimes living in a state of siege, it seemed to me important to reconstruct Woolf in that guise, so that the kind of book Anna English ends up having to write is very different from the one she set out to write.

AC: You've mentioned some of the parallels between Canada and Ukraine: both producers of raw goods and importers of expensive goods; "like Canada, in relation to the powerful US, and also like Quebec in Canada: Quebec before the Quiet Revolution, where you had to speak the language of the conqueror in order to be heard at all" (*The Green Library*, 181). As you point out, Ukraine has had few defences and many invaders. What did it mean to you to explore your Ukrainian heritage in *The Green Library*?

JKK: First of all, I was careful to write from the point of view of a character who is only half-Ukrainian, and who doesn't discover that she has this ethnicity until she's a grown woman. She realizes that her ethnicity is not a voluntary affair. I couldn't start writing that novel until I'd come to terms with my own sense of who I was, nationally, ethnically, culturally. I also couldn't start to write it until Ukraine had become an independent country. I had friends who'd gone to Ukraine when it was under Russian domination, pre-glasnost, and it was like entering an occupied country. Your freedom of movement was severely curtailed; you could not speak Ukrainian to the people in the streets, even if you were in a city like Kyiv. I went in 1993 and spent a few days in Kyiv on my way to a conference in Germany. I'd grown up thinking this city was the home of my heart or the heart of my home, this ancient mother city of Ukraine, and to be there was phenomenal, in November when you didn't see the sun at all, with leafless trees and white mist. It was also disconcerting, at a time of economic distress. It was quite extraordinary, very moving, very alienating, but certainly something I wanted to write about, but which I couldn't dream of doing without some empirical evidence.

AC: Did you feel there was an element of translation going on? In *Constellations* I had a sense that you were sometimes constructing conversations in English that would have been spoken in Acadian French. How have linguistic traditions affected your work?

JKK: I have a very promiscuous and irresponsible attitude to languages. I love speaking them. I had some German in High School. I always loved the idea of switching between languages. It's like having a variety of perspectives you can see things from. You can view things with a kind of acuity that a unilingual perspective doesn't give you. There's always that element of wrestling with language, trying to get some kind of approximation. All writing is translation.

AC: There have been challenges to white middle-class feminism in Canada by critics who feel that race is inadequately represented. You seem to challenge the victim paradigm in your work, and yet there are characters like Mariette, the part Micmac girl who is rendered sterile by a bungled abortion. This situation recurs with a character in *The Green Library*. Is this a way of talking about specifically female problems?

JKK: I think from an early age I knew that History with a capital H is nightmare country, and that if you're a woman you're doubly vulnerable: you can be raped, or you can be rendered sterile because the master race doesn't want you contaminating their boys. I also have the character Jeanne in "April Showers" in *Transfigurations*, who is an Acadian woman actually packed off to a convent, which is the only way that she could get an education. She finds that the constrictions are too severe, leaves the convent, marries her high school sweetheart and has seven kids, then complains bitterly to the friend who's become a high-class lawyer and finally had one child that abortion is easy if you're rich, but if you're living on the French shore in Canada it's different. There I was trying to talk about issues like women's right to determine their biological destiny.

AC: The economics of abortion?

JKK: Yes, but also trying to create this character Jeanne who has a degree of agency that Mariette never has. I wanted to have a story where there's a very powerful Acadian woman who does not have an education, but who is very capable, outspoken and earthy. I wanted to create a character who's a corrective to the victimized figure.

AC: What were you trying to achieve in the very complex narrative structure of *The Green Library*, switching between a number of different geographic and temporal settings?

JKK: I was going back a little to *Constellations*, my first novel. I think you always learn how not to write a novel with your first novel; you do it the hard way. I knew that I was an outsider living on the French Shore, with no means of access into the culture. It was the same thing in *The Green Library*. I was dealing with people from extraordinarily disparate parts of the world. Therefore, when I got Eva to Ukraine I wanted to have people who were not part of her story except in the most vestigial way. I also wanted to get a sense of cultural and national rupture. I guess it's a fairly hackneyed contrivance to have two lovers from different countries who come together, especially if there's a marriage. I was going to end the novel with a decisive rupture between Eva and Alex, two completely different people whose histories would never allow them to come together, but I decided that would be a cop-out and I'd much rather have a relationship that continues, through the obstacles of distance and difference.

As many critics have theorized, we only know ourselves through others, through an understanding of otherness. I wanted that to be a strong component of Eva's character. I also wanted moments when the children in the story occupy centre stage, as for most of the novel they are on the fringes. There are many different tellers and listeners of stories, with their own takes on story itself, on where stories begin and end. I wanted that sense of heterogeneity and also of multiple lives going on at once, overlapping and infringing. I also wanted to bring in a formative aspect of Ukrainian culture as I knew it, which was a diaspora culture, but which reflects certain truths about Ukrainian cultural experience, the extreme overvaluation of the male, and the extreme undervaluation of the female. Daughters really have a very circumscribed role to play.

AC: Would you explain your use of the term "transcultural" as opposed to "multicultural" writing? I see that the term is generally used for writers after the seventies in Canada, but could even Susanna Moodie be considered "transcultural" in that she was resting her British gaze on the rough backwoods of Canada.

JKK: I wanted to use the term "transcultural aesthetics" in contradistinction to "multicultural writing". People talk about multicultural literature, but with very few exceptions the people who write the books are not multicultural at all. I'm very much in favour of a radical multiculturalism, and I certainly think that most multicultural practice today is highly problematic, but I would certainly be hugely opposed to trying to go back to some mono- or bicultural model.

AC: I liked your argument that a multicultural society in Canada has often been squeezed into MacLennon's "Two Solitudes" model.

JKK: I found Neil Bissoondath's book, his vituperation of multiculturalism, extremely bizarre, most disturbing and peculiar. His desire to go back to some paradigm of Canadian identity that I can't see ever existed. For me "transculturalism" has a strong connotation of crossing borders, crossing boundaries of things normally kept separate.

AC: In one's writing, or in identity?

JKK: In one's national or cultural construction. It's the opposite of ghettoization, opposite to a kind of mosaic where every mosaic is cemented into place.

AC: The official policy sounds a bit like South African retribalization for the homelands policy, where the Zulu had to live in one "homeland", the Venda and Sotho in another; here's your ethnic niche.

JKK: If you're a transcultural writer, you're writing across the borders and boundaries. If you were a transcultural Susanna Moodie, you'd be writing not just back to the mother country and not just to the future daughters of the Empire. You'd be writing across the borders that divide you from your Irish servants or your Irish neighbours, and you'd be trying to break down some of the stereotypes that keep you so hostilely and retrogressively divided. To me Moodie is not transcultural; she's very keen on keeping up all kinds of class and other special distinctions.

AC: Is it a matter of audience, then; she's writing back to a home British audience about an exotic place called Canada?

JKK: But it also relates to subject. If you're a transcultural writer, the kind of characters you're creating, the kind of experiences you're dealing with, are ones you know will be of interest not just to your own little cultural community. And despite what Dionne Brand and Himani Bannerji have said in highly polemical interviews, the fact that Dionne Brand reads so many writers other than Black writers, and that she's now recognized through the Governor-General's Award and the Trillium Award, make her an important writer whose work speaks to Canadians of whatever original ethnic derivation. You can't say, "I write only for my own people." I guess I feel very strongly about that because I grew up in a community that has this shibboleth phrase "our own". You keep to your own, and your own is always better.

AC: The Afrikaners in South Africa have a similar phrase, "ons mense" (our people), but of course that phrase was always racially and exclusively defined.

JKK: The transcultural writer is one who kicks down that wall of "our own". It doesn't have to be a banner that you're hoisting, but you're not writing for your own community and not just for Canadians. You're writing in a global context where to be displaced, to be an immigrant, a migrant, is one of the most common human conditions and experiences.

AC: Would this have something to do with immigration law? With more visible minorities coming into Canada at a certain date, creating a constituency of their own and putting certain pressures upon Anglo-Canadian sensibilities?

JKK: That's certainly true. With the shift in the sixties, changes to immigration law and the introduction of the points system. No longer were you privileged if you were a British citizen, you were judged according to your capacities, through there were certain very strong prejudices built into the system. Those with higher education and socioeconomic background were privileged, unless the labour market needed people who didn't have those qualifications, as with Displaced Persons. After World War II, if you were in a DP camp in Europe applying to emigrate to North America, you calloused your hands and dirtied your fingernails, so people would never dream you were a writer or a lawyer or a dentist. You had to pass yourself off as a manual labourer.

What I've found most disturbing about immigration policy recently is the attempt to change the law so that only immigrants who can speak French or English with a degree of fluency will be allowed into the country or given preferential admittance. This strikes me as an incredibly retrogressive move, and if applied to my family in 1936, my grandparents, mother and aunt would not have got into this country at all. I find this new trend a most lamentable so-called "leap forward".

AC: Do you feel any affiliation with the line of women writers, if it is a line, that links Margaret Laurence, Alice Munro and Margaret Atwood, Canadian women writers who have written about growing up in small Ontario or Canadian towns, a "lives of girls and women" tradition?

JKK: It's interesting that the Canadian writers I most admire of a certain generation are not transcultural, though Mavis Gallant could be considered transcultural: Alice Munro, Margaret Laurence, Margaret Atwood, all for different reasons. With Gallant and Munro their artistry is extraordinary, though the sense of the world through their work is very different. There's the passionate curiosity they both have, their power of observation. They're both astounding. They should be declared national treasures, and feted. Mavis Gallant should get a huge stipend, a quarter of a million dollars a year, just for writing.

AC: You're saying that Canada still underrates its writers?

JKK: I'm thinking of the Japanese tradition of declaring certain writers to be living treasures. The Irish do not require their writers to pay income tax, a degree of civilization we've yet to reach, despite the existence of the Giller prize. Think of someone like Margaret Laurence, being a woman writer at a time when it was extraordinarily difficult to be one, especially if you were a woman of great imagination and generosity, which she was. I also feel extraordinary respect for Laurence's sense of her oeuvre, that sense that she had only so many books to write.

Margaret Atwood is extraordinary too, with the sharpness of her intelligence, and the role she's played in remaining in Canada when she could so easily have gone elsewhere, by the example she's provided of someone who is utterly cosmopolitan and is yet utterly Canadian. And she's a very political person, as well as being a political writer, who is able to write quite remarkable fiction that is political in the very best, most comprehensive sense of that term. Hence the way she's able to intervene at given moments, when the *Globe and Mail* features a piece about Quebec, or a letter from Atwood about the underfunding of the arts in Ontario. She does make a difference, and that is an extraordinary role to play.

I've obviously felt an empathy with Mavis Gallant because she's spent so much time in Europe and also because so many of the writers who've influenced me have been European. I don't feel that as a writer who is Canadian my horizons are entirely bounded by Canadian writing, although some of the best writers in the world right now are Canadian.

AC: Or are certainly displaced in the transcultural way you describe.

JKK: But certainly Conrad, Woolf, James, Akhmatova, Paul Celan are as important to me as Jane Urquhart, Carol Shields, Michael Ondaatje. The wonderful thing is the *embarrasse des riches*. There are so many extraordinary writers out there, and so many of them happen to be Canadian. It hasn't just happened like that; I remember when Michael Ondaatje won the Booker Prize there was an issue of *Time* which stressed the Transatlantic. The author spoke about the transcultural phenomenon and said that Toronto had become one of the publishing capitals of the world precisely because of this, with writers like Rohinton Mistry, who lives in Toronto, and Ondaatje.

AC: Thank you so much for your time. Would you read your poem from *The Green Library*, "Kindness of Strangers"?

"Kindness of Strangers" from *The Green Library*

Out of this maze of streets a stranger walks towards me.
Unpremeditated yet expected, he has perfect manners
and a pair of wings, dwarfed and misshapen,
clotting the place where his heart should be.

Together we walk to a bridge over a great river.
We do not cross but stand looking down
at drifting boats, at streetlamps sunk
like eclipsed eyes.

I open my coat and show him my birthmark,
mud-thick, the colour of dead blood.
He puts his mouth to my breasts;
the stain turns to wine, pours clean away.

His wings break like wishbones
in my hands. Now there is nothing between us.
We stay a long time on the bridge,
the river rising, till it carries us off,

together,
in different directions.
Everything solid has vanished.
The air fills with smoke like rain.

There Will Be Gardens:
Alice Boissonneau

Alice Boissonneau was born in Walkerton, Ontario, a third-generation Canadian of Irish background. Her grandfather became a schoolteacher, then a journalist and editor of St. Mary's newspaper, *The Argus*, after her family moved to St. Mary's. Her mother was also a schoolteacher, and Alice studied at Victoria College, University of Toronto.

She became a social worker in the late 1940s and observed the urban poverty stricken world of Scottish, Cockney, Slav, Jewish and Scandinavian immigrants in Toronto. Social work in Toronto was a shock to a young woman from a sheltered rural Ontario background, and she began the detailed notes of what she observed in the journals that later became the stuff of her fiction. After a few jobs in Toronto she moved west to B.C. and was employed in hospital rehabilitation work at the Vancouver General and the Provincial Mental Hospital.

After her return to Ontario and her marriage in 1961, Boissonneau began her writing apprenticeship while her husband was a land-use researcher in the north and they lived in a trailer. Later they moved to Cannington and she completed two novels there. She later moved to Guelph and lived there until her death in 2007.

Boissonneau's first novel, *Eileen McCullough* (1976), shortlisted for the Books in Canada First Novel Award, records the everyday life and problems of young people during World War II and aspects of the vast social movement of people from Ireland to Canada. Her second novel, *A Sudden Brightness* (1994), evokes the consciousness of a seriously depressed woman awaiting release from a wartime Vancouver hospital. She has also published an evocative memoir of Toronto life and urban impressions, *There Will Be Gardens* (1992). More recently she has been working on a set of stories based on memories of her early life in Walkerton.

Boissonneau's fiction is a lucid, compassionate and visually detailed record of the post-Depression decades of urban Canadian life. Because of her life as a social worker, she has been especially involved in depicting the inner world of poverty and economic struggle in Canada.

She writes with a steady moral vision and social compassion that irradiate all her writing and recall central European traditions of the novel and of naturalism. Because she works from detailed observations in her journals, her fiction has a brilliant impressionistic quality in the sensory detail. Her sensitivity to mental suffering and depression, an infrequently recorded aspect of the everyday life of immigration and poverty in Canada, marks a fictional record that always moves toward hope and illumination.

Interview with Alice Boissonneau

AC: Much of your writing seems to draw on your knowledge of places and people gained as a social worker. How has your life as a social worker influenced your writing, in themes and style? Do you feel there was a connection?

AB: Yes, I do, because I didn't really start writing until after I started social work. I came from a southwest Ontario background, between Stratford and London, where the land was considered to be the best in Canada, and people did not really suffer as much from the Depression. When I came to Toronto and started my jobs as a social worker, it was a very shocking, in-your-face experience of observing people with babies living over dusty fur stores on Queen Street, and babies whose bottles of milk were kept on windowsills over the street during heatwaves. That was how they had to live. I hadn't seen that before. Perhaps what really strikes home to a writer is what makes up the subject matter for them.

AC: Your writing is set in wartime or postwar Canada in the forties and fifties, and you use the phrase "bearing sons away". The crisis of your novel *A Sudden Brightness* turns on the breakup of a marriage caused partly by the separations and stresses during World War II, and the pregnancy and abandonment in Eileen *McCullough* also relate to wartime absences. Are the mood and the artistic method of your fiction shaped by your experience of World war II?

AB: Yes, I think everyone during that period was very affected by what was going on in Europe during the war. The part about "bearing sons away" didn't really have that wartime meaning. It implied the passage of time, of generations, and the walks that I had taken around all those streets in southwest Toronto, which I went through for at least a year, because of some of the characters in the first novel, *Eileen McCullough*, which I wanted to set in Toronto and where working class people – I've learned that in large plants like Massey-Harris they were mainly British – were just taken off the street.

AC: There's quite a time lag between the time settings of your novels and their period of publication. Would you comment on the key changes between then and now?

AB: In the background of Southern Ontario where I'd lived, and left to go to university at seventeen, people did not write novels, that was in my youth. Perhaps they read novels at Christmas, such as Dickens. I was thus groping quite a bit. There is an apprenticeship in any of the arts, or in any craft that you learn, and I had been trying to learn the craft of stories and complete sketches. I had to learn how to write the first novel, and I was not really very adept at it.

AC: Who did you learn from? Were there particular people?

AB: There was one friend who lived down the street from where I was in Toronto. She was very friendly, Eleanor Godfrey – she's since died – but she was older and was connected then with *The Canadian Forum* magazine. We became friends, but I don't believe, though she was very talented herself and very skilled at literary judgement, that she knew how to help me. The one conviction she gave me was that she told me, "You're a writer," and no one had told me that before. That was a step up in that respect. I had to find what they call, rather tiresomely, "your own voice". I lacked confidence, so it took a long time. Then, when I was working in hospitals as a social worker, I loved the jobs, it was rather like being pressed between the pages of Balzac; every five minutes you were talking to someone who was confronted with some horrendous problem. They had only two weeks to live, or there would be people coming in off the street who wore rubbers lashed onto their feet with elastics, and your mind was just swimming with impressions. I made notes on weekends, on Sundays, wrote little sketches and notes, written often in phone booths and hotel lobbies. But I didn't have the time in which to really complete that material until later, starting with the period when I was moving around northern Ontario in a trailer and my husband was working at land use research. Hence there are those different lags, here and there.

AC: I think it's contributed to your work, because it gives a sense of a very layered past to the memories of the cities you write about. To me it's given richness.

AB: The idea came to me when I'd walked for nearly a year around the southwest part of Toronto, near Massey-Harris and the old Queen Street Hospital. I needed to know what the streets were like in different seasons, for background information for the novel that I was working on, *Eileen McCullough,* and also about characters. I talked to people in their houses about their pasts, but in doing so I realized there were layers I was walking upon, of past times, and that was how that feeling came to me about the layers of streets.

AC: Your work deals so much with the subjective experience of women's lives, with grief, pain and loss. You've mentioned that you lacked confidence as a writer; is that because women feel that men should be the storytellers of society? I know that "woman writer" is a questionable term, because we don't call male writers "men writers", we just call them writers. What role do you think gender has played in your work?

AB: In part there's a simple reason that I wrote about women. Possibly you feel closer to your own gender in describing situations, but also I remember when I was working in the Out-Patients of the General Hospital in Vancouver, it would come to me, and this is another angle, that men had a hard time too. They would have to go out and take buses through sleet, and come to work, and they could not change their jobs easily, and they needed the reputation that would keep them receiving a steady income. Whereas it was easier for women to change their jobs and, probably quite incorrectly at the time, I felt that women who were in the home had a somewhat easier time, making jelly and looking after children. But that was quite incorrect, I realized that later. And women didn't really have much voice either.

AC: I was thinking about women in wartime. In your writing the things that women often suffer from in ordinary life are intensified by war. For instance, women are usually socialized to wait for events, but in your fiction they have to wait, because there's a war on, there's no option, and also because your focus is often on institutionalized women, or in dire poverty, in intolerable circumstances, those characteristics of passivity are intensified.

AB: Women did not have a voice, really, as much as men did.

AC: And was that one of the reasons for your stories and themes?

AB: Yes, that was one of the reasons. And then also I felt that there were divisions, not only between women, but in working in the Provincial Mental Hospital, and later working as a volunteer in a rural Ontario old age home, there were these other arbitrary divisions made by society generally, that categorized people: Oh, these people in this hospital are all stashed away, let's not think about them. They're different from us, and they're very peculiar. And the old people have no interest, a lot of them are senile.

AC: You were also overcoming the stigma of mental illness?

AB: I found that patients were given most help not so much by social workers who had to do all kinds of professional, practical things for them, but by volunteers who came along and would drive them out with peanut butter sandwiches, away from the grounds, and treated them like human beings. I felt that was so much needed.

AC: How do you see the relationship between your fiction and European traditions? You refer to Blake, Goya, Bach, and Van Gogh. You use the beautiful phrase, "childlike images of blinding innocence", which reminded me of Blake.

AB: I just thought of that out of my head. That was mine, but it's from reading, of course.

AC: Yes, but it's almost like a description of Blake's work, too. And also your characters have a kind of "blinding innocence", I think. And you mention Goya and "a mirror of murky times". I found your writing has such a detailed realism, but it's wedded to a spiritual or visionary tradition. Have you travelled or lived in Europe, or is your relationship with European traditions more of a literary affinity?

AB: Yes, I would say there's a kind of literary affinity. I was very keen on the work of James Agee. Are you familiar with his writing?

AC: No.

AB: Well, he wrote *Let Us Now Praise Famous Men,* about the people in the American south who lived in dreadful houses and suffered a great deal picking cotton, and yet they were individuals. He characterized them in a very poetic and wonderful way.

AC: Your style is such a sensitive barometer. I wondered how anyone could possibly remember in such detail what the facades or roofs of buildings looked like, and also render them subjectively. Many passages of your writing are like grainy photographs of Vancouver and Toronto, very visual. Do you paint, or what shaped this particular impressionistic and detailed vision of places?

AB: I've looked upon that as a bit of a weakness, because plot never seemed to interest me that keenly, and I seemed always to be captured by a particular impression or situation, and to want to get that down more than anything. And when I did try to write plot more, I never quite succeeded, and I wasn't as happy about it, whereas in this way I was thinking about it directly.

AC: Well, I didn't miss the plot. I think writers create their own forms.

AB: I think so too.

AC: You seem to defamiliarize the familiar, rendering the urban environments that we take for granted as strange and visionary, and I think this works with your thumbnail sketches of people too. In *There Will be Gardens,* you speak of "pictures held in the mind like rooms", but you also mix in historical details of Toronto, its houses and past citizens, a whole layer of British imperialism and grand houses. For me it worked as a foil to the current realities you were describing, but also as a stylistic interweaving of fiction and history. How do you see fiction in relation to social history?

AB: In walking along these streets in order to provide background for the first novel I wrote, *Eileen McCullough,* I did quite a bit of research into the archives, found out who the people were who had lived there. For instance, near Dundas and Shaw, I walked along with this older friend of mine who'd been brought up in that area, and I could see it through his eyes. I learned all kinds of little lore from the streets, from people talking, for instance, the baby brought up from a ravine on Shaw Street was raised as Ravina Shaw, wonderful things like that.

AC: It also struck me as part of your social commentary because all those grand old houses would have had one household, one family in them, and the contrast with six or seven people crowded into two rooms becomes part of the social critique. That memory is there of the grand colonial homes, but look at how people are living now, crushed together.

I liked your phrase, "the everyday resistance movement of the human spirit", which you are demonstrating in your characters but also describes the mode of your writing. Your obsession with getting all the details down reminded me of Alice Munro's description of the town of Jubilee, in *Lives of Girls and Women,* in which she writes of a need to recapture every detail of the place. You've used the phrase, "a hedge against loss"; do you see writing as "a hedge against loss"?

AB: When I was working in the Out-Patients section of the General

Hospital in Vancouver I was so knocked out by the courage of people there. You'd see people every five minutes; it was very crowded and very hectic. People who knew they would die within a month, and they would talk to you. I felt the way they were overcoming their obstacles was amazing; I could never get over that. Their courage was just so incredible. And I think that is true of people in general. I never got over the courage people showed in a day to day context.

AC: Your writing is a tribute to those people.

AB: Oh yes, yes, it certainly is.

AC: I think you told me you write from life rather than inventing a great deal. Would you say that has been a dominant mode for the Canadian novel?

AB: Probably not. That may be a weakness on my part, though in the novel, *A Sudden Brightness*, most of it is completely invented, but then I would imagine scenes; I would go back inside a situation and attach it to that person or situation.

AC: In *A Sudden Brightness*, do you set up that situation to show that people can get through bad bouts of depression and misery?

AB: Yes, but as well as that, I didn't want to write about the true-blue schizophrenic in a hospital. I wouldn't have the temerity to do that, and I wanted to show this was a girl who's had what they call an ordinary breakdown and was groping in her mind toward the future, and the patients were absolutely confined to the grounds. Their journey, their plot had to be in their minds, because their only companions were the other patients or doctors. But I did feel she was trying to cope in a way, by reviewing her past, so she could make sense of it, so it would help her move a few steps forward.

AC: Yes, I see now. That's how you structure that narrative. It starts off in the mental hospital, and she gradually works over the past again. Right at the end she's released. That explains the narrative form.

AB: That was rather difficult, because in other novels people have jobs, they get married, they move from place to place, but these people in the hospital grounds, all they have are their thoughts in their minds, and they're confined to the companionship of other patients, so it was rather difficult to do that.

AC: And then you have the internal narrative of her previous relationships with her family and her husband as a memory, a reconstruction.

AB: Yes.

AC: Who are the writers who have been important for you in Canada?

AB: Alistair MacLeod. I think he's a very wonderful writer. Do you know his work?

AC: Yes, I do. He has the same kind of focus on poverty, ordinary life. I heard him read a beautiful story about a man in the Salvation Army or some kind of hostel; the description of the setting was wonderful, very moving.

AB: He carries a story so beautifully, and includes all the necessary details, and makes it so alive for you. And Austin Clarke is also a wonderful writer.

AC: I've just read his recent novel, *The Origin of Waves*. Marvellous. And then he's a link with the immigrant world, because I notice with a lot of people in *There Will Be Gardens*, the reason they're living on the fringes is that they're immigrants and often "non-European", or what are now called "visible minorities", so they're struggling. You have a good phrase about "the dogged dream of the new country".

AB: I've just recently read the report from PEN, on imprisoned writers, and I felt very conscious of those situations.

AC: In South Africa, there's a huge tradition of that, writing either in prison or about prison experiences in retrospect, because imprisonment for political opposition has been so common. My imagination is steeped in images of imprisonment.

AB: About a year ago they had Nelson Mandela and Bishop Tutu on television, and discussed how they interviewed people for the Truth and Reconciliation Commission. It was a question of "Can they forgive?" They would show a black man whose face was being pushed into a sink of dirty water and left there till he was nearly choking, then he'd be lifted out and choked again. How could the family forgive actions like that?

AC: I liked your phrase, "everyday resistance struggle", because South Africa has been so embroiled in the political resistance to racism and apartheid. It's political resistance that's been more directly presented, but what I'm seeing now through your work and Alistair MacLeod's is a type of social resistance, which comes from wanting to register the lives of those who are struggling at the bottom of the social hierarchy, and there are quite a lot of them. And then of course there are historical phases in Canadian history when it's been worse, and your fiction chronicles some of those phases. I felt that way when I first read Margaret Laurence and Alice Munro: everyday but profound conflicts and experiences were the centre of attention. There was a kind of normality, and the normal became mysterious, which was different from the special racial problem of South African fiction.

AB: Have you read Mary Jo Leddy's book, *At A Border Called Hope*? She's an activist nun who has worked with refugees, and she has a consciousness of the people who've been taken for granted, the whole process of refugeeism and immigration, and things that have been wrongly dealt with in Canada which are now coming to light.

AC: Having been through the whole process of immigration myself, I think that it must be terrible if you don't have the English language, because it's painful enough even if you do.

AB: Apparently they're put on welfare. They're not allowed to work, and then they wait not knowing, sometimes for months, whether they'll be shipped back to the same country. A very enlightening book.

AC: The topics you deal with sound depressing: grief, sadness and loss, but the effect of your work is not at all depressing. There's a sense of hope and gaiety that comes from your mastery of a detailed style. Also your narratives move towards a definite lifting of heaviness, an illumination. You mention working through minutia until there's a moment of vision. Reading a novel of yours feels like reading a long poem. Do you write poetry at all?

AB: I wrote very bad poetry as a teenager. Structure was a difficulty. When I started apprenticing myself I wanted to draw everything together in great unity, and I found it very difficult to break into plot and make the plot work. And finally I found ways to do it in a personal fashion that seems to have worked.

AC: So you do a lot of drafting and correcting?

AB: Yes, a lot.

AC: Because I read *There Will Be Gardens,* too, as a kind of novel, as one narrative, though it's printed in episodes or sections with titles. That was an effect you wanted to get to then, of one narrative?

AB: Yes, yes, I probably did, because the ending ties it together. It just happened by itself.

AC: Would you comment on the difference between writing short stories or sketches and a novel?

AB: I began writing in a random way, notes, which later grew into short sketches or stories, put down in reaction to shocks experienced during my early day-to-day training in the profession of social work. In contrast with the short stories, though again I was driven to record by an image of the environment, for the novel, *A Sudden Brightness,* a different structure was needed. From the experience of working as a member of the rehabilitation department of a BC psychiatric hospital I felt the impact of its enormity, which dictated a more complicated structure of stages. These would allow for a longer search for meaning, to show the descents and the dark parts, and with more than one character.

During the months spent at the institution, I became familiar with the attitudes of outside society, which stressed the bizarre nature of appearance and behaviour of the many schizophrenics warehoused in the giant buildings and coming from different parts of Canada. They could not recognize that behind each patient might lie a simple story.

I chose in contrast a somewhat ordinary young woman as the main character, who had suffered a breakdown from life's disappointments. Divorced from her husband, separated from a loved teenaged daughter boarded out in Vancouver, and with her discharge imminent, she is struggling to avoid a return to the east and her unsympathetic family. The different kind of setting dictated a special narrative direction. The patients, penned up in Day Rooms or confined to the grounds, had only the company of fellow patients; unlike individuals in outside society, they were not able to apply for a job, acquire new friends, or change to new quarters. Any action or movement of necessity took place only in their own thoughts and minds.

A structure of images was needed to reveal an unfolding, designed to take place in short random periods when the young woman was able to be alone and free on a bench in the grounds, sketching views of the mountains. She develops then, without planning to, slowly coming back from her childhood and marriage, leading up to her present situation. Slow insights rise out of this. Interchanges with other patients also contribute.

In contrast the short story is required to have a singleness of focus, describing one incident, at times allowing for a few relevant ramifications that may add to the incident. The novel in its longer search for meaning and structure of stages, with possibly many more characters than the central one, is able to show changes with the passing of time.

AC: Could you comment briefly on the new collection of short stories you are currently preparing?

AB: In moving to Guelph four years ago, my attention was drawn back to the town of Walkerton, where I was born, now in closer proximity. I became interested in attempts to record memories of the place, in the shape of sketches and stories, which are in the process of being completed. I hope they will provide another picture of past western Ontario times.

AC: Thank you for your time and commentary. Would you read a section from *There Will Be Gardens*?

"Winter" from *There Will Be Gardens*

She lives on Queen.
Queen is the boundary for her.
She goes west on Queen,
East on Queen,
But seldom north.

And there is something like an empty cellar about Queen,
You go along and along,
And what you look for
Never comes and never happens.
It is like being blind.

Snow marks the street like holey gloves
And the street-car marks a seam down the middle,
Straight and long.
Winter sands the store windows and scalds the eyes
With bitter gusts.

I hear the little lambs crying.

"Kawaiso" and Japanese-Canadians: Joy Kogawa

Joy Kogawa was born in Vancouver in 1935, a third generation Canadian of Japanese ancestry. Her father was an Anglican minister. She and her family were victims of the Canadian government's policy of internment and dispersal of Japanese-Canadians during World War II. In 1942 some 21,000 people of Japanese ancestry, 17,000 of whom were naturalized or Canadian-born citizens, were uprooted from their west coast homes and resettled in the BC interior and in Alberta. "Kawaiso" is a Japanese phrase used to comfort children.

Kogawa is the author of several volumes of poetry: *The Splintered Moon* (1967), *A Choice of Dreams* (1974), *Jericho Road* (1977), *Six Poems* (1980), *What Do I Remember of the Evacuation?* (1985), *Woman in the Woods* (1985), *A Song of Lilith* (2000) and *A Garden of Anchors: Selected Poems* (2003). Her three novels are *Obasan* (1981), *Itsuka* (1992) and *The Rain Ascends* (1995). She has also written non-fiction: *Gently to Nagasaki* (2016) and children's literature: *Naomi's Road* (2005) and *Naomi's Tree* (2009).Kogawa has also published poetry, specializing in the long poem, such as "A Song of Lilith" (2003), which she read at a special performance in Guelph.

Obasan (1981), Kogawa's powerful first novel, is a lyrical recounting of the inner history of post-war Japanese-Canadian experience, and the moral and spiritual quest of a young girl to confront and understand her family's suffering in World War II. The novel won much well-deserved acclaim, the Books in Canada First Novel Award, and the Canadian Authors' Association 1982 Book of the Year Award, among others.

Itsuka (1993), Kogawa's second novel, shows Naomi, her protagonist, gradually caught up in the Japanese-Canadian community's struggle for redress from the Canadian government, and shows how a morally activated socio-political movement evolves in modern Toronto, and within the stresses and divisions of networks of families and friends.

The Rain Ascends, Kogawa's novel for children, explores the psychological and moral predicament of a young Anglo-Saxon girl who discovers her minister father has abused young boys sexually.

Kogawa's fictions probe uncomfortable moral dilemmas and emotional quandaries that spring from complex problems in modern political and social life, especially the wartime experience of the Japanese-Canadian community and memories of the violent devastation of the nuclear bombings of Japan. She deals with issues of war and violence, intimate sexual abuse, the oppression of minorities in supposedly liberal democracies, religious doubt, and the cultural diffusion of Japanese heritage in Canadian society. Her writing is morally relentless and yet lyrical, sensitive to family hopes and rituals, cultural differences and social assimilation in Canada, and infused with a courageous spirit of resilience.

Interview with Joy Kogawa

AC: Thank you for your writing. Your novel *Obasan* meant a lot to me when I first arrived in Canada from South Africa. It seemed to speak to my enormous sense of loss of a whole country and community. I read an excerpt from it at the first conference I went to in Ontario, at the University of Waterloo. As this is Remembrance Day in Canada, and we have war losses in mind, I should like to ask you about *Obasan*. I read it as a quest for a mother. The narrative moved toward recovery of a lost mother, and that recovery seemed to mean uncovering the meaning of the atomic bombing of Nagasaki, which is where the narrator's mother and so many others were destroyed. That narrative movement toward personal and national trauma was very powerful for me as a reader, and probably for many others. How do you feel about that novel and those World War II events now?

JK: Before I answer your question, I find it interesting that you are from South Africa, because I'm currently reading an autobiography by Willem Verwoerd. He talks abut his struggle around his South African name, as his grandfather was the architect of apartheid. He discusses his own desire to make reparation, to be true to his own deepest impulses and the need for justice. I'm interested in this basic desire for home that is at the root of so much of our human longing.

AC: Was the writing of *Obasan* therapeutic for you? Did it deal with your emotions around that Japanese-Canadian World War II experience of dispersal and loss so that you could let them go, or do they continue?

JK: Concerning the girl's search for her mother, I think that the longing we have for home, for a primary bond, is almost a metaphor for a human being longing to be at home in the universe, to be one with God, or simply to have an at-homeness. I look back on that book, and on my particular life – we all have these particular journeys we go on – and I now see that I had to tell a peculiar story of a peculiar people at a specific historical time. There was a particularity about that, but I now see all of that as a metaphor for the larger human journey that we're all engaged in, no matter what stage of history we're living through in the present. That was then, and life has not stopped, nor do I go back to that time and see it as mirroring something unique. I look upon something beyond that. Today my engagement is with the current lostness of people who do not have money, and then the lostness of people who do have money. The struggle around Mammon, or the principles around Mammon, those principalities and powers against which we war, and which have so powerful a presence in our lives, engages me a lot today.

AC: Would you talk about the relationship of Japanese culture to Canadian culture? *Obasan*, unlike your next novel *Itsuka*, seemed to me to look backward to the original Japanese culture, and to be about ancestors, about Japan's relationship with the United States as well as Canada. You give wonderful details about Japanese culture: the sense of humour and decorum, a respect for concrete details and the body, for certain rituals such as the bath rituals, and a sense of humility and service. Do you see those qualities in Japanese culture as surviving within Canada, or as having blended with a broader Canadian culture?

JK: We're all a product of our environment, and my parents came out of a particular country that had developed forms and rituals which became the world they grew up in. These rituals they brought with them to this country, and remained within them, and were passed on. As soon as they are passed on to another generation, that generation has many other values that become part of their identities. Although those values, such as respect for education, may be passed on, they can be described in other ways, and seen as Western values as well. Certainly I grew up with Eastern values, and a sense of the Japaneseness of things, or the Easternness of things. Nevertheless I have a great deal of the Western influence, and particularly the Middle Eastern influence via England, via the King James Bible. That all becomes part of who one is, so it's hard to say, when one tries to trace the deepest values within oneself, where they originally come from. All human beings have at root some common virtues and values, however expressed, for example the value of human kindness. It may be differently expressed, but we all agree it's good to be kind.

In the Japanese culture the silent strong would be valued, whereas in the Western world forthright speech is valued. There could be conflict there, as to which has greater value at any given time. Value differences need to be constantly described and explained to prevent misunderstanding.

AC: *Obasan* seemed to be about the value of silence, a lyric about silence.

Would you talk about your responses to nature, particularly in Alberta? You describe Japanese fishermen transposed from the West Coast to the Prairies, and often describe the tall grasses as a kind of sea. Was your own experience of leaving Vancouver for the Prairies mainly one of dislocation?

JK: The very first short story that I published was called, "Are There Any Shoes in Heaven?" It was about a little boy and his family who had been in the mountains and had loved the mountains, and then they were on the Prairies. This was a Japanese-Canadian story, but I called them the Parker family, and they were tall white blonde people. In that story there was a great sense of longing to be back in the beauty of the mountains and a hatred of the Prairies. In my childhood experience I had great, fond memories of Vancouver, so I had always wanted to go back to the city. I loved the city; it was my first place, the joy and fun of the city, the elevators, escalators, Christmas lights. When we moved to Slocan I missed it all. I longed to go back to Vancouver. When we went to Coaldale, Alberta, a place without trees, and with wind, it felt like hell to me. I did so want to go back anywhere but out there. Above all I wanted to be back in the mountains, in Vancouver.

I did not really come to terms with being in the Prairies. But in recent years when I have gone there, I've gained a new appreciation of the love people have for that place, if they were brought up there. I can remember going into the mountains with a group of children born on the Prairies, and they kept saying the mountains were so monotonous, all those trees and rivers were so boring in comparison with the Prairies. Because in the Prairies you would drive along and see a house over here and then something else over there; it was always different. I found their perspective so different. Then there was a friend from up north, talking about the paradise it was up there, and the beauty of the snow. I think where love is, and where your home is, there is beauty. For me, that was not Alberta, not until much later.

AC: Do you see any parallels between Japanese-Canadian and First Nations experience in Canada? I'm thinking about the loss of land and resources, and a struggle for compensation that centres in land and dwelling places. In South Africa we had massive forced removals of whole communities, which caused terrible suffering over many decades. Do you see parallels between different groups within Canada, or internationally?

JK: I think people who've been oppressed or identified as undesirable develop an abiding anxiety, a sense of non-belonging and worthlessness, and the struggle to come out of that is tremendous and lifelong. Some people never get to feel they can go anywhere. I remember as a young woman always wanting to find that parts of town that had Chinese restaurants, where I could go and feel at home, and not feeling at home anywhere else. It took me a long time to feel I could go into those big hotels with plush carpets and sit down. I know what that insecurity feels like.

Now I think people who've been there and have come out of that, have choices. They can either cease all identification with their former powerless group, and reject those people, and try to be like the people they imagine really belong, or they can stay connected. The Native people who have the burden of identity of the "unwanted" or "despised" have a tremendous struggle. And Japanese-Canadians who went through the political process of attempting to publicize their story and gain redress would have developed political wings, as they say, a form of new consciousness. After the redress movement many joined in alliance with native peoples, and created an identification and moved on in a kind of solidarity. There are others who continued to move away from their origins, to dissociate themselves from everything poor or downtrodden in an attempt to become as rich as possible. These are the psychological realities common to many immigrants. When the mainstream group identifies any other group as less than desirable, then you have that gap, and have to overcome that gap one way or another.

AC: Your poetic narrative in *Obasan* incorporates many historical details, a journal in the form of letters by Aunt Emily, and ends with a historical document, the Memorandum sent by the Co-operative Committee on Japanese Canadians to the House and Senate in April 1946. I notice that *Itsuka* also ends with an official document, the Canadian Government's acknowledgement of injustices and the violation of human rights involved. Did you write *Itsuka* in order to show how anger and activism are born out of injustice? In *Obasan* there was a contrast between Naomi and Aunt Emily concerning activism and political involvement.

JK: *Obasan* was written after a long period of time in which I had written only poetry. It was my first attempt at writing a novel and was written without a great deal of consciousness. It arose out of dreams and instincts, like my poetry. After *Obasan* the pen fell from my hands for a while, and then there was a sense of urgency about picking it up and writing again. I was thinking about the subject of *The Rain Ascends*. Initially, in planning another novel, I was thinking of writing about three different priests, the way certain moral choices were played out in their lives, in their choices and judgements. I was developing the personality of Pastor Jim. Father Cedric was going to be another character. I wasn't sure where it was going. While I was doing that work I got highjacked into the whole redress movement. And so *Itsuka* took a turn at that point. Perhaps it should have been two novels, one purely about the redress movement, and one about the other topics. I then wrote *The Rain Ascends*, another book that came out of things my mind was working on. But I think that in writing about the redress movement in

Itsuka it was more a journalist's imperative than a novelist's imperative that directed the book. I'm not sure how well it works. I've not read it. And so it sits there, as this thing.

AC: I like it very much, because in tone and setting it seemed to take a leap into modern urban Canada. The voice is a modern Canadian voice. I liked the way you covered some of the same ground as *Obasan* but in a much more humorous and accepting tone. This told me something about the historical load that had been lifted in your first novel.

How do you feel about other Canadian writers, especially writers like Rudy Wiebe, for instance, who also writes historical fiction and addresses political and social history in western Canada? I didn't see much reference to other Canadian writers in your earlier interviews.

JK: Generally I read around the topic that is engaging me at the present moment. I'm always engaged by moral struggles. I'm not a good reader. I used to be. When I was a child I read voraciously. I read everything I could get, which was not a lot in Slocan, Alberta. There was more available in Coaldale. I took a course in Canadian literature at one point, and read several Canadian books at that time. The one that stands out in my mind is Buckler's *The Mountain and the Valley*. I haven't really had much of an appetite for this country's writing, so to speak. In the sixties I was very eager to think about questions of good and evil and guilt. So it's true that I don't know much about the Canadian literary scene. It's such a bonded community, though, that we all know each other in some way. I know the new writers less well, because I haven't gone to any Writers' Union meetings recently. But the people of my generation at the Writers' Union and League of Canadian Poets, we know one another well. So I don't really know what we're doing. I need the scholars to tell me things.

AC: In *Obasan* there's an interesting interweaving of a narrative of children's sexual abuse with ethnic exploitation and racism. The subject of child abuse is expressed most clearly in *The Rain Ascends*. I think this was a very brave thing to do, to address this topic which is so painful for everyone, in every community. It's a very difficult topic to write about, to think about, to process psychologically. In *Obasan* I thought that Old Man Gower worked as a kind of analogy, another form of evil, on a personal level, but similar to the larger story of Japanese-Canadian relationships during and after the war. Was the writing of *The Rain Ascends* a way of of confronting ghosts? Was it another attempt to deal with the same human conundrum, the paradox of good and evil? What brought you back to address the topic in a full-length novel?

JK: I think that we're all struggling all the time to understand what it is to be human and how our journeys unfold and what signposts we have along the way. I don't really understand the ramifications of something like child abuse, but I know it affects the imagination in some way. It affects us basically, at the core of what we are, what is allowed, who we become, but I don't understand how these things work. We have Freudian theory and various schools of psychoanalysis, which tell us these things, but I think I was trying to understand some of this stuff, and I still don't. Therefore it is an ongoing journey. Whether it expresses itself in a group, ethnic sense or in an individual context, to me they're both part of trying to unravel a mystery.

The narrator, Millicent, says that a sword in the bowels is not usually there to set one free. That novel tried to unravel some of the entangled bits of the human psyche and put a face on evil. We don't overcome evil by burying it, by not seeing. Why am I writing such work? Right from the earliest days of my life I had a hunger to know the truth. I remember as a small child praying daily to know the truth, whatever I meant by that. I just remember praying for it. I still do. I still want to know. I still hunger for something. I get baffled by our capacity for escape, to keep running on the surface of our lives. I get impatient with that.

AC: I wondered if the fictional expression of child abuse wasn't an attempt to address hypocrisy, because child abuse is often covered by social hypocrisy, just as the treatment of the Japanese was covered over by political hypocrisy. I noticed that when you described the split that happens in the young girl in *Obasan*, it was done in terms of a lie. It wasn't so much the invasion of the body that was at the centre of attention, but the idea of a man going out in public and presenting a public face of decency when privately there was atrocity. That was my understanding of it. Does that make sense to you?

JK: Yes, that does. That's helpful. I always like it when someone comes up to me and explains something I've done. I really do. Often one becomes simply the vehicle for something that somebody else understands. Thank you.

AC: How close do you feel to your protagonist Naomi? Women writers in particular often work through this slightly distanced female alter ego. I have written short stories, too, and I used the name Alice, which partly draws on fable. You used the character Naomi in three books. Would you talk about your relationship with her, and about your children's book, *Naomi's Road*?

JK: I felt like Naomi when I was writing *Naomi's Road*, and after I'd finished writing I felt more like Aunt Emily. That was a few years later. It was as if Naomi was written about, and then Naomi remains static, because she was there, and I was no longer her. But she had been a part of me and still is. But in real life I could move on. Perhaps that is one of the reasons for writing. It enables one to move on in some way. Having felt more like Emily I could move on as well. I don't know that I ever felt much like Obasan.

AC: There is a subdued story about spinsterhood in your work, which is also a gender issue. I really enjoyed your humorous accounts of perceptions of single women in small town Alberta. The religious fundamentalism you described and the narrowness of perception were very informative and entertaining. And of course there's a lot of love between women in your work, especially women in families: aunts, grandmothers, mothers and daughters. How do you see the relationship between gender and ethnicity in Canada? Or perhaps you'd like to speak more specifically about spinsterhood, because in *Itsuka* there's a beautiful movement toward companionship, and happiness, a pleasure in no longer being alone.

JK: It's a strange thing, but if circumstances in my life hadn't been what they are, I would probably have remained a spinster. That is, I think I would have had relationships, but not married. I don't know. I've never thought about that particular question. No one has ever asked it before.

AC: Perceptions of spinsters, which are also perceptions of the Japanese in Alberta, seemed to be part of your story.

JK: What's interesting to me is that many of the Japanese-Canadians who were dispersed after the war didn't have close associations with each other, because they were in fact scattered. Marriage outside of the group was not very common. So there is a relatively high percentage of people, a little older than me, who were of marriageable age at that time but never married. I think it would be interesting to know what happened there, what the values were that prevented them from really going out and exploring and rebelling and getting married, which normally happened with a young adult. But I think Naomi is the kind of character who was raised to obedience and to honour the old. So she would have been one of those typical Japanese-Canadians who would not have been married. I haven't consciously spent much time thinking about questions of gender, women and men, although I have a close-knit group of women friends who are feminists. That seems to be the world I imbibed, but I've not done a lot of reading on those topics. That hasn't been a central, driving motive for me.

AC: You've explained something to me there, how dispersal would have affected gender relations. When people are scattered in that way, it's obviously going to affect marriage patterns too. I hadn't thought about that.

How do you understand the Japanese experience of labour, with the beet industry in Alberta during and after the war? I've just attended a conference at Brock University and heard a paper arguing that the World War II treatment of Japanese simply gave another form to a racism that was already there in Canada, and perhaps another form to earlier anti-immigrant feelings, sometimes quite explicit. Do you see that historical experience now as one of racism, or as arising out of wartime fears in Canada, or as masking labour needs? You've now had experience living in Toronto as well, and *Itsuka* is set in Toronto. Do you read Canada as having been more racist at some times than others?

JK: Back in the 1940s there was a certain climate, and a certain acceptance of practices by the government that we would not tolerate today, the wholesale removal of people from their homes and scattering them hither and thither, establishing policy that said they should never be a community again. A policy where the watchword was assimilation, integration, was not respectful of diversity at all. It was a whole different way of viewing what they thought was for the good of the whole country. We imbibed that view, and each of us felt we should be the only Jap in town, and inconspicuous. Having our movement restricted in that way, and having understood that if a city did not want us to live there, then they had the right to refuse us: that was acceptable policy then. There were only certain places we could go, and the only places we could go was where there was a need for our labour.

All of that I now see as a heavy-handed control over the lives of groups of people, not taking into consideration the wellbeing of those people one has control over. We were just so many pawns. One grows up feeling helpless, that one is a pawn and that the state is all-powerful. The wishes of the majority constitute the only reality that we can consider. That becomes the way things are, and you grow up believing that and not questioning it, until someone comes along and says: "Let's question the whole idea." Then things change and you come to another set of beliefs, and can go on to other ways of seeing.

I know that as a child my only reality was that my labour, and the labour of my Japanese friends, was amazing. To look out at a field which looks endless, to start with a hoe, and to go down that whole long row, then to start with the next, and there's no end in sight. The only thing you can do is look at the one plant in front of you and go on and on and on all day long, any you get faint. I look back on that now, and it may seem weird, but I actually think I learned so much from that. It has given me such endurance that when I am facing a difficulty or work that needs to be done, and I know I have to draw on my powers of endurance, I can say, "Well, it's not as bad as the sugar-beet fields." And I can say, "You just do tasks one at a time, and then you get through them." Perhaps this is a Pollyanna philosophy, but I feel gratitude for the experience, because it has given me tools for survival.

AC: I emigrated from SouthAfrica in 1990, so of course when you talk about models of endurance I think of Nelson Mandela and all of the others who suffered for so long in prison or various forms of arrest and detention to reach the goal of democracy in South Africa. Those people are my inspiration. You do somewhere mention having read Mandela's *A Long Walk to Freedom*. And you're now reading the autobiography of one of the descendants of Hendrik Willem Verwoerd, one of the major architects of apartheid. There's been a complex generational struggle in South Africa, and I see your writing about the Japanese-Canadians as one of different generations, moving toward redress. Would you like to comment on this global struggle for dignity and freedom? Was it the Japanese-Canadian redress movement that made you understand the global struggle?

JK: Yes, I think the redress movement did give me a great understanding of the ways in which we are all connected in our different struggles for equality, dignity and freedom. Knowing that what we do here is connected with other struggles over there enables us to carry on and not feel completely isolated in our work. I am moved by the stories of other people's struggles and am also inspired by them. They can serve as models for us, but I think it's only when we experience, within our own lives, and our own selves, our own struggles out of some prison or dungeon that it becomes a really learned lesson. We can read about someone else's struggle, but I think our capacity to be moved to act comes out of our own personal lives.

In terms of South Africa, I heard that Nadine Gordimer had left the South African Writers' Association. What would be the reason for that?

AC: With South African writers, the resistance movement sometimes led to much ideological control of literature, to prescriptive attitudes, something of a cultural desk. Many writers had a sense that they were now being ideologically programmed in another way. They didn't want to write propaganda of any kind, whether Nationalist or anti-apartheid. You deal with that issue as well, your sense of not wanting to write to any programmed aim, that programmed writing is not what works as literature. In South Africa much of the literature has been organized around the political system because it was so oppressive. Some protest was overt and superficial, and there was a reaction against it at the time of political change, a sense that inwardness and private lives might return to the stage, a celebration of the ordinary. When you read the literature historically, you see that those protests were a necessary part of their time. The rhetoric of African resistance, the Black Power rhetoric was also necessary at the time. Did the redress movement produce any overt protest writing from other Japanese-Canadians?

JK: Politics tends to be blinkered. The need to win is so powerful a force that you cannot take on the "enemy's" point of view sufficiently to have a well-rounded picture. It's difficult to step outside one's own position. In that sense, there is propaganda, and in *The Rain Ascends* I was trying to get to the other side. By the time I had finished *The Rain Ascends*, which is not a political work, I was able to come out of that with a capacity to see Hitler differently. And I think that enriched me, because I would not have imagined that outcome would have been produced by that journey.

AC: Was it because you had dealt with the child's perspective in *The Rain Ascends*? Sometimes going back to childhood vulnerability gives one a different adult perspective.

JK: Being able to enter the reality of the victimizer or the reality of someone who would love the victimizer, which was the situation of Millicent in that novel, enables another perspective. Often, in situations of conflict, we have the polarity of victim and victimizer, whereas the reality of both victim and victimizer is very complex and is surrounded by whole communities, interchanging players, who can walk between. In politics you usually have competing partners and oppositional, conflictual interactions. Then you have propaganda: not the desire to know the truth but to win. And when the desire to win is stronger, then you have propaganda. I'm sure a lot of propaganda was written during the redress movement from within that community and from outside. The question is not whether you can stand outside that, because I think you can not, if you are a person of conscience. You get pulled in and make a choice. Sitting on the fence in those situations is quite damaging. Part of you sits on the fence and part of you acts in spite of that.

AC: In relation to South African political change, I have worked toward greater Canadian and global investment. I can see that investment would benefit the social and educational infrastructure. Education was destroyed by the apartheid policy of educating Africans for inferiority.

JK: I met Willem Verwoerd at a Calgary conference, which was on the topic of reconciliation. He had been working for the Truth and Reconciliation Commission. It was very interesting to me to hear of this hope for the future in South Africa, and the different perspectives of those engaged in the process. There was so much that we need to learn from, here in Canada, in relation to the aboriginal peoples. Recently there was an article about the highest suicide rates in the world being among the Inuit, and that phenomenon definitely needs to be examined, so we can understand what's going on and why, how deeply the self-hatred has been learned and from what sources. I think the better we understand these things, from large and small perspectives, the further along the way we can go, together.

AC: The aboriginal experience in Canada seems to me one of colonial intervention as well as segregation. It's an ambivalent process. The European message seems to have been: "We want to 'civilize' you, but you must live apart from us." And so in a strange way the movement for aboriginal rights still seems to rest on sovereignty claims. It's unlike the South African struggle, which was for a political voice for those already economically integrated, to a large degree, in the cities. Africans were already there; they were living in the cities, the labour that built the cities and worked the mines, but they didn't have any political voice or vote. And of course they suffered from huge economic disparities. In Canada, there's pressure from Quebec, and First Nations claims still seem to depend on separateness rather than community or integration. What is the political benefit of claims to autonomy and self-government?

JK: I don't feel I can really talk about that either, because I haven't been in that situation myself. I can take stabs and guesses, but it would be like a man talking about women's issues.

AC: It has to do with an attempt to understand the particular tensions between assimilation and integration in Canada.

JK: I think that's quite a good way, to keep thinking and asking about it. I know that if there has been a situation of abuse in a native community, the whole community gathers around in a healing circle. The abuser is able to be confronted directly by the people who have been harmed, and there is then a capacity for healing. That's an entirely different approach to the one we have, which is to lock the person up and isolate him. They would want to carry on with a justice system that is more enlightened and humane, and get people out of these horrible prisons into communities where there is some love and understanding.

AC: A listened to your reading, last night, of your long poem, "Lilith", with great pleasure. Would you say more about your own responses to spirituality and religion? *Itsuka* takes a turn toward recording the lives of priests, religious leaders. I noticed that in your "Lilith" poem, towards the end, there was some repetition of the word "trust". That word does not come up much in your earlier fiction. You don't speak about forgiveness of reconciliation. In South Africa, as you know, there was an official Truth and Reconciliation Commission after the apartheid era ended. There was such an enormous sense of damage that it had to be publicly addressed. People had to tell their stories and get rid of some of their grief. In your work there seems to be a dialectic around truth and forgiveness. As you say, when you were a child it was the truth that you wanted, but sometimes trust has to proceed without knowing everything, without knowing the truth. I thought there was a dialogue between those two principles, truth and trust, in your long poem last night.

JK: For many years, since my first real crisis with the question of good and evil, trust became the dominant word, the watchword, the signpost of my spiritual journey, and it was a trust in the benevolence of what

Willem Verwoerd calls "my caring presence". I trust in that "caring presence", and, in the face of human betrayals and our own delusions, if I did not have a deeper trust I would be a leaf in the wind. I get blown around by things anyway, but without that trust I would be insane. The question for me is: how does one move on with joy and confidence and meaning right through to the grave when the feeling of trust may have gone, because one is overwhelmed by the reality of evil. How is that to be experienced?

I think there is some secret about the word "sacrifice" that we have rejected in our day. In the "Lilith" poem I want to have a different Lilith than the one of traditional myth, and to undergird her with her own journey toward trust. There may be something preachy about the end of that poem; it will probably undergo more changes. There's so much to say about that, so much to uncover and discover, that I don't know what to do at this point in my life. Right now I'm so engaged with my community work that I'm not writing, but I still feel it's all a part of the journey. And whether I'm feeling that I'm trusting or not, I know that I am. It's always there, underneath.

AC: Would you say that your writing has been one way of reaching that deeper trust?

JK: I know I came to the insight that I was able, in spite of knowing nothing, to trust in benevolence. The writing was simply a tool in the journey, and it continues to be that. If I were simply to write for some other reason, for entertainment or gain, it wouldn't be very satisfying. It would lose its purity, and I would fear that. I want it to remain a tool for the journey.

AC: Would you say a little more about your community work? Is it about poverty issues, or immigration?

JK: It's definitely about poverty issues. The last line of *The Rain Ascends* reads, "The journey will lead into the abundant way." Because the journey had started with the dream that the goddess of mercy and the goddess of abundance were the same, that somehow one could not come to a state of mercy unless there was a great deal of abundance in one's life. Mercy was not expected of the poor person, only of the king. So I knew that the next leg of my journey would mean looking at systems of abundance and scarcity. Through that I stumbled into the worldwide currency movement, the community currency system, which is a community of people trying to write another story than the dominant economic one.

AC: Thank you very much for your time and conversation. Would you read the conclusion to your novel *Obasan*?

From *Obasan*

"This body of grief is not fit for human habitation. Let there be flesh. The song of mourning is not a lifelong song.

Father, Mother, my relatives, my ancestors, we have come to the forest tonight, to the place were the colours meet – red and yellow and blue. We have turned and returned to your arms as you turn to earth and form the forest floor. Tonight we pick berries with the help of your sighted hands. Tonight we read the forest braille. See how our stained fingers have read the seasons, and how our serving hands serve you still.

My loved ones, rest in the world of stone. Around you flows the underground stream. How bright in the darkness the brooding light. How gentle the colours of rain."

Obasan's eyes are closed as she continues kneeling on the bed, her head bowed. In the palm of her open hand is Uncle's ID card. Her lips move imperceptibly as she breathes her prayers.

Through the open doorway I can see the faint shaft of light from the kitchen across the living-room floor, straight as a knife cutting light from shadow, the living from the dead.

I tiptoe out to the kitchen and put on my cleanly scraped shoes. Aunt Emily's coat is warmer than my jacket. I slip it on over my pyjamas and step out to the car. The engine sounds loud in the predawn stillness. As I drive, the drops of moisture on the windshield skitter to the sides of the glass and disappear.

By the time I reach the coulee, the sky has changed from a steel grey to a faint teal blue. I park the car at the side of the road in its usual spot and wade through the coulee grass as I did with my Uncle just a month ago. The stalks are wet with dew and the late night rain. My pyjamas and shoes and the bottom of Aunt Emily's coat are soaked before I reach the slope.

I inch my way down the steep path that skirts the wild rose bushes, down slipping along the wet grass where the underground stream seeps through the earth. My shoes are mud-clogged again. At the very bottom, I come to the bank. Above the trees, the moon is a pure white stone. The reflection is rippling in the water – water and stone dancing. It's a quiet ballet, soundless as breath.

Up at the top of the slope, I can see the spot where Uncle sat last month looking out over the landscape.

"Umi no yo," he always said. "It's like the sea."

Between the river and Uncle's spot are the wild roses and the tiny wildflowers that grow along the trickling stream. The perfume in the air is sweet and faint. If I hold my head a certain way, I can smell them from where I am.

Restless Western Women: Aritha van Herk

Aritha van Herk has published five novels: *Judith* (1978), about a woman hog-farmer in western Canada; *The Tent Peg* (1981), set in the Yukon; *No Fixed Address* (1986), where a panty-saleswoman sells her wares across western Canada; *Places Far From Ellesmere: a geografictione* (1990); and *Restlessness* (1998). She has also published several volumes of criticism and non-fiction: *In Visible Ink* (1991), *A Frozen Tongue* (1992), *Mavericks: An Incorrigible History of Alberta* (2001) and *Audacious and Adamant: The Story of Maverick Alberta* (2007).

Her work, translated into many European languages, has won her the Seal First Novel Award (1978), the Province of Alberta Achievement Award for Literature (1978), and a prestigious election to the Royal Society of Canada (1997). She has also taught Creative Writing and now teaches in the Department of English at the University of Calgary.

Van Herk's genre-breaking fiction creates characters from ordinary walks of life: bus-drivers, secretaries and cooks, and takes them on journeys to escape restraint and the conventional limits of storytelling. She has a talent for describing Albertan landscape features, farm life, and the landscapes and isolated communities of the north. Her writing shows that women can take on many challenges in life and survive well. She creates strong autonomous women characters and deconstructs conservative myths about women in Canada.

In a recent talk in Guelph she spoke of restlessness (also the title of her 1998 novel) as a central feature of Canadian life, in immigration, internal migrations, and the adventurous imaginations of Canadians who keep reinventing the nation. Regions, she said, are as much different places of spirit and imagination as physical locations. Canada's most valuable feature is its ability to take in strangers from all countries and walks of life.

Van Herk is at the forefront of women writers in Canada who question not just patriarchal attitudes, but also the inherited genres and plot directions of traditional European fiction. All of her novels challenge the traditions that insisted that female heroines should attain family and fulfillment in marriage, and a reconciliation with society. The forms of her fictions are turbulent and uneasy, overturning readers' expectations and literary conventions. This postmodern playfulness questions the relationship between social conventions and literary decorum.

The central qualities of Van Herk's fictions stem from a combination of practical Dutch-Canadian working-class survivors and literary sophistication. Her novels are anchored in Albertan localities where the family farm has been dismantled. Van Herk's women explore the boundaries of stability and restlessness.

Interview with Aritha van Herk

AC: You're a first generation Canadian of Dutch descent, yet you seem to define yourself against Alberta as a region, and you articulate a dissenting feminist perspective against certain Canadian literary traditions. Does your Dutch heritage mean anything to you; do you see it as having shaped your writing in any way?

AvH: I think you cannot escape your heritage even if you try. Probably for the first ten years of my writing life I tried very hard to escape my heritage. Having been raised as a Dutch Calvinist, a fairly strict upbringing that I was happy to escape from when I left home to attend university, I was not eager to re-inscribe that in any way. On the other hand, I discovered very quickly that as you have been inscribed so will you inscribe, whether you try to escape it or not. So there are elements in my texts that really do reflect my heritage: the stubborn assiduity of my characters, their perpetual wandering, which is a feature of immigrants, and various other elements that are visibly and linguistically Dutch. I have a particular approach to language which stems from knowing Dutch before I learned English.

AC: You spoke Dutch at home?

AvH: My parents, during the first years of my childhood, didn't apprehend English very well; they were recent arrivals.

AC: So you were raised speaking Dutch at home and learning English at school?

AvH: Exactly. It wasn't until the middle of my school years that I was fluent in English.

AC: And you think that the restlessness idea also comes from your immigrant background?

AvH: I think from immigration, yes. Not necessarily because we came from the Netherlands, but from the fact of immigration.

AC: You've often mentioned the western Canadian literary tradition as predominantly male, and burdened with patriarchal notions of women's places and roles in society as well as literature. Has your attitude to these traditions and writers changed over the process of your own fictional creation and professional career? I know you've published on Robert Kroetsch's writing. Have the works of Robert Kroetsch and Rudy Wiebe, as two major Western Canadian authors, been models as well as anti-models for you? Was Kroetsch one of your teachers?

AvH: Robert Kroetsch was not one of my teachers, though I wish he had been, because his writing has taught me an enormous amount. And his attitude towards story, towards narrative and language, has been a great influence on me.

I can remember with wonderful clarity the moment when I knew it was possible for me to be writer. And it wasn't a sudden inspiration as much as a recognition of genealogy. When I went to the University of Alberta, the first English course I took included one of his novels, *The Studhorse Man*. In that novel there's a wonderful scene were Hazzard Lepage lets loose all the horses from the slaughterhouse who escape across the high-level bridge. From where I lived I could see the high-level bridge from my window. And this was the first time in my life – I was very young, seventeen or eighteen years old – that I held in my hands a book that described a scene I could actually look at. And I don't think we can underestimate that moment. For writers who live in London or Paris or New York it's a common occurrence. But for a kid on the Prairies it was extraordinary. It was absolutely convincing and very moving for me. It was an emotional moment.

So his influence on me has been very positive and benign. The traditional way the West was written, however, through the genealogies of Frederick Philip Grove, Sinclair Ross, W.O. Mitchell, Robert Kroetsch and Rudy Wiebe, these five mammoth men, is at the same time a disheartening one. It's terribly male and sexist and patriarchal and has not taken into account, in any shape or form, the perspective of a woman. So I've had to negotiate all of those visions. There have been others, Sheila Watson's, for instance, but in fact those are five massively powerful visions to argue with or against. And I have found myself all my life doing a lot of that, because in some strange way I'm one of the first women to come out of that tradition, which seems very peculiar to me. At the same time, there is a tradition of western Canadian women's writing. Margaret Laurence is a part of it, so is Sheila Watson. So it's a strange friction. I do believe my writing acts in many ways as Kroetsch's books do, but I think that isn't so much that we share a world-view.

AC: Is it because you're both experimental writers?

AvH: Yes, but we also grew up very close to each other. Now, he's much older than me, but the landscape that shaped his childhood also shaped mine. He grew up not twenty kilometres from me, right on the edge of the Battle River. So I think it has something to do with local vernacular, a particular history, and the whole crosshatching of a community that's very similar, and so that has infiltrated our work as well. He isn't eager to share that notion of the Prairies as a drought-ridden, miserable dust-bowl either. He's a powerfully ironic writer, full of playfulness and fun, and his heroes are women. The men are all abominable failures, or as one character says about his male characters, "Men are a bunch of useless assholes." So in a strange way I've always adored the writing of Robert Kroetsch because he's so quotable.

AC: I can see the similarities there.

AvH: Whereas though I've studied with Rudy Wiebe, I have no similarities to his writing, though he's a good friend. But I'm not interested in the ponderousness of his writing.

AC: Or in his historical vision?

AvH: No, not at all. We don't share a similar world. And the same is true of W.O. Mitchell. The romantic view of the Prairies that has now been picked up by Sharon Butala is not of interest to me. I'm a much more cynical urban writer than either one of those two. And Grove I consider a total imposter.

AC: He was literally an imposter, wasn't he?

AvH: Yes, he was. He was pretending to be something he wasn't. And Ross is perhaps the next most interesting to me, because of his attempt to take on a female voice.

AC: It seems that you became much more experimental later. *Judith* is much closer to the conventional novel form. So you took courage as you went on, I suppose.

AvH: And in content as well. Very much so, the rural setting in *Judith*. But if you read it carefully, and begin to see the pigs as the narrators of this novel, it has the potential for subversion.
AC: Oh yes, it has great potential for subversion. I wasn't saying it's not subversive. But it's not subversive in form as much as your later work.

Your work is much concerned with mapping and spaces, with restlessness as opposed to settlement and stasis. Does this concern stem from an oppositional attitude to settler traditions in Canadian literature? I notice that your work contests the notions of moralism, of the sublime, and romantic notions of nature, which could be considered features of early female settler writing, like Susanna Moodie's.

AvH: In a sense I am terribly antagonistic to the settler writing tradition, perhaps because I live in a place that emulates a frontier, though it wasn't a frontier, and because so much of my own restless exploration has taken me to the north, which is not at all a settler world and never will be. It is a nomadic world, and will continue to be one, in every sense of the word. So yes, I get very impatient with Susanna Moodie's desire for parlours, and how to manage chambermaids.

AC: And with the moralistic? Because I think your work explodes a lot of moralisms.

AvH: Some people have called it amoral.

AC: I don't think I would go that far.

AvH: Thank you, thank you. I'm saved.

AC: One supporter is not enough.

AvH: I'm not interested in literature as morality. I'm interested in literature as telling a great story, as being subversive, as reflecting a kind of bizarre euphony that we share with the world, and then I think that too often the writer doesn't listen so much as decide the way the world should be. So my writing is like overheard conversations in lunch-rooms and beer parlours, in a strange way. I want to record frictions and cacophony.

AC: The books are great page-turners. There's a real narrative energy that takes one on. And I don't think that's a quality in early pioneer writing, partly because of form. It falls into an episodic structure: now I'll tell you about the settlement, now about our Indian friends. Whereas you cultivate that narrative that takes you on in a kind of excitement.

Some critics have discussed the mythological patterns of your work, especially the reclaiming of female divinities to counter the patriarchal traditions of most religions. I can see that in Judith you've used myths of fertility, and Circean myth. How consciously are you aiming to challenge a Puritan ethic in this way, or is this simply a way of steeping fiction in female myth?

AvH: It's not mythology per se, so much as that I have a desire to retell the stories of women that have been effaced. Not erased, but effaced.

Whether it's the story of Circe in *Judith*, or the story of Jael in *The Tent Peg*. I use many biblical heroines who have been interpreted by biblical scholars in ways I find unacceptable. Now of course this revisionist approach of mine is not necessarily enjoyed by all, but it gives me narrative pleasure. Because it isn't so much the feminist reclaiming of narrative space for me, as that I think women's stories have an endless quality, and a labyrinthine capacity, that we still haven't figured out how to use. We still fall, as women writers, toward the male master narrative. Trying to usurp that, to stand it on its head, to make it work for us is a great challenge, and one that I'm not sure we've yet really grappled with. At the popular level there's an effort to reclaim it, but I'm not sure I want to reclaim it. I almost want to explode those stories.

AC: The patriarchal biblical myths?

AvH: That's right. And the way women have been used within them to shore up the master narrative. And the same goes for something like *Anna Karenina*. The way I used that story in *Places Far From Ellesmere* is not because I think Tolstoy is not a great writer. He's a marvellous, fabulous writer who invents this incredible character, that he then does not know what to do with. So he must kill her. He has no literary choice. But this is not about my geographictione, *Places Far From Ellesmere*, criticizing Tolstoy. It's that I want to know Anna in a different way. I want to take her even farther than Tolstoy did, which some people think is a real transgression, and other people are able to take pleasure in.

AC: So you're trying to give your female characters a kind of power by relating them to a tradition of strong goddess-like figures.

AvH: Yes, I'm trying to give them a lot of agency, an ability to manage their own lives, which is tremendously empowering.

AC: It did occur to me that most of the goddesses you refer to are pretty vengeful ones. They're the enveloping spider-figure, or they knock tent-pegs into men's skulls, or have the power to turn them into swine. So in that way, too, you run counter to the popular mythology, which is that goddesses are passive and sit up in the clouds.

AvH: Me heroines are never benign. I don't apologize for that.

AC: Your fiction challenges many stereotypes of women and takes female protagonists into male terrain, male work spaces, and sometimes into male clothing and identity, as in *The Tent Peg*. Is this a way of saying that there's no limit to what women can do, or a literary symbol of the shifting parameters of sexual identity? Or both? You seem to want to create women who take their sex "neat", like men, or as men are presumed to do, who are often promiscuous without guilt. I'm thinking mainly of *No Fixed Address*, which has a husband waiting at home while the wife takes her pleasures outside of marriage. Is there a danger of simply inverting the stereotypes?

AvH: In many ways that novel engages with many parodic elements. Of course, you can say Arachne is a reversal of the male picaro, who runs around getting into trouble, and she behaves in exactly the same way. In a sense that becomes part of the parody. But for me it was extremely important to play that out to its fullest extent. I did not want to impose on her behavioural restrictions that male picaros have never enjoyed.

AC: And that male authors have seldom given to women?

AvH: Exactly. The female picaros invented by male authors, whether Moll Flanders, Fanny Hill, or Thelma and Louise, have been punished for their transgressions. Not one of them ends up alive and unreformed. Those are the two choices they have: to die or reform. And I did not want, within those parameters, to reform this woman or to kill her. And that is why people are so uneasy with her, because they think she's not really following through as a typical female character, because she's never sorry, and that's great, because I wanted to push it past that envelope, so that her story at the end is for her an act of empowerment. She has gone through every possible experience, and there's nothing left except to disappear, but she does not die. She's not going to be killed as a result of behaving so badly, whether it's promiscuity, or the thefts that she commits, or the murder she appears to have committed as well. She's an unrepentant rogue, and that was extremely important for me to explore, I guess because women have so often been turfed into repentance when they have simply not been interested in it.

AC: I would say then that you aim to unsettle your reader, which I think you do, but this rather contradicts your idea that the bond between the writer and reader is an erotic one. I think you subvert readers' expectations a good deal. In *No Fixed Address* you even build in a reader figure, or perhaps another writer figure, who is trying to find Arachne. So you've built into your text a reader who wants closure, and that creates a very interesting dialectic in that particular novel. But it does shift us away from the idea of reading as an erotic experience, which you emphasize in your essays.

AvH: But the erotic is display. I don't think of the erotic as peaceful or static. I think of it as deeply perplexing.

AC: Yes, that's true.

AvH: So for me, unsettling readers is exactly what I want to do in order to seduce them. You're absolutely right, but readers don't see it that way. They see seduction as something that makes you comfortable. But again, I suppose I want to subvert expectations of all kinds. My refusals and nasty little games and my knitting needles in the side are often very uncomfortable. I'm aware of that. They're also uncomfortable for me as a writer.

AC: They must be. It must be difficult to work around the traditional closures of narrative, because where do you take your characters? So your work certainly fits the mode of deferral. You're a deferral specialist. Nobody's ever fully seduced.

AvH: Always. That's what desire is about.

AC: But some people are fully seduced.

AvH: Once desire is fulfilled it no longer exists. It exists only as long as it is deferred.

AC: It exists until the next seduction. But there has to be a seduction.

I'm interested in your understanding of the "Western" genre in Canada and what subverting it might mean. In some ways you seem to draw on a tradition of action and adventure, to move your protagonist to new frontiers (though in the north), but you also speak of female Westerns as being devoted to interior space, showing women as universal citizens. Could you expand on that? Is the north the place in Canadian literature where one escapes the frontier mentality?

AvH: Well. The north is the ultimate frontier. You're right about the paradox. For the male writer the whole notion of the Western, or the frontier book, is about going beyond all possible confinements. For the woman writer, for my women characters, there is that notion of escaping all possible confinements, but at the same time recognizing that this is an impossibility. Arachne goes to the end of the canal road, which is where the roads in the north end. The road just dwindles into nothing. That's a real historical place. You can drive only so far. But Canada has been geographically mapped by the geodesic survey so that when she comes across the peg with the geodesic notation on it, she knows that although there will be an end to the road, there will be no end to the male mapping of the world, so she is trapped within the very spider web she has escaped. There's that constant paradox; it's endlessly oxymoronic.

AC: We can't escape culture.

AvH: Of course not. And that scene is there to signal that though she may run from him, and the city, and the confinements of domesticity, she cannot escape the master narrative that writes her, which is the way that women are socially constructed.

AC: Yes, because she's also in love with him. There is that tension. The love and the cultural construction seemed to me to be in very significant interplay at that point in the story, because it's a kind of behaviourist mapmaking.

AvH: Kroetsch has spoken of this relationship as a reversal. Thomas Telford becomes the wife while the woman goes off on a horse. So he represents gentle domesticity, but he also represents a very privileged man, in stark contrast to Arachne who has no privilege at all. So it's a combination of freedom and confinement. We're always looking at the parameters of those two things and how they work together.

AC: The mapping theme is very rich in that novel.

There's a lot of humour, fun and entertainment in your fiction, and I see affiliations with popular writing: farming romance (*Judith*), comic art and travellings salesman's stories (*No Fixed Address*), camping or prospectors' yarns (*The Tent Peg*), the murder mystery, assignation with death story (*Restlessness*). Is this part of an attempt to broaden the readership for Canadian fiction? You mentioned that *No Fixed Address* had a high circulation, about 12,000 copies sold.

AvH: It's still a literary readership. I try not to make my books inaccessible. Despite being an academic now, I'm a person from a working-class family which nevertheless believed books can give you a grounding in the world. So it's very important to me that people can read these books on many levels. That someone can read Judith as just a good story, and *The Tent Peg* and *No Fixed Address* and *Restlessness*: does he kill her or not? Many people have read that book in just that simplistic way. And that's fine. Because narrative is an archeological dig, a multi-layered thing, and for someone who knows the story of Arachne there's a richness to *No Fixed Address* that's just different from the readers who read it as a story of a crazy promiscuous bus-driver-cum-panty-saleswoman, as a rakish rogueish figure whose travels they admire and love.

It's fascinating to see your readers' responses. I heard recently from a woman who wrote and said she was a sign-painter, and she has an entire interpretation of the novel worked out as a sign-painter, because of course there is a sign-painter at the end of the novel when she's driving on Vancouver Island. This woman really was a sign painter, and she had a totally different reading. And one woman used to sell "legs" pantyhose to all those little towns on the Prairies. She had a wholly different reading. There's an urgency to write a story that anyone can reap something from.

AC: That works terribly well. But I also think it's healthy for Canadian literature when writers create accessible works, because novels like *The Double Hook*, which seems to be claimed as the first modernist work, are fairly literary. I don't know about Robert Kroetsch's readership, but it's good to break down the boundaries of a minority elite readership.

AvH: His new novel, *The Man From the Creeks*, is a retelling of Robert Service's *The Shooting of Dan McGrew*. By telling the story of "the lady that's known as Lou" he tells the story of the Gold Rush to the Yukon. So he's been a real model for me.

AC: He's a wonderful writer. The narratives work at so many levels.

Your focus seems to be on the rebellions and self-assertions of young white settler women, on subverting gender stereotypes. How does your writing relate to traditions of aboriginal culture and it's political claims to land and rights? Is your version of the female trickster derived from indigenous traditions? Arachne certainly seems to have some features of the indigenous trickster figure, in her slyness and abundant energy, and shape-shifting.

AvH: In point of fact, my writing doesn't relate at all to First Nations experience, because I think that's territory that is best claimed by aboriginal women. I can only write about the world that I have access to. For all that I have First Nations friends, and though I know their writing well, I don't think it is my job to meddle in their story. So I pretty much stay away from it. Arachne is not so much modelled on the trickster figure as on the tradition of Cervantes and *Don Quixote*. And when I was writing *No Fixed Address*, I was reading all of those old picaresque novels.

AC: So it's a European tradition that you're drawing on.

AvH: Very much so. But I think there are also cross-cultural affiliations. The trickster story may be a First Nations story, but it has resonance in other cultures. And I don't know it as well as I know the European picaresque story that I made it my business to investigate. I'm fascinated by the writing of First Nations women particularly because I think they're trying to reinvent an authentic story, one that will authenticate their own experience and will articulate the multiple worlds they know. And so far for me as a reader it's a wonderful thing to read their work. But as a writer I don't think that's a territory I'm familiar enough with to begin to apprehend.

AC: Have you had First Nations readers responding to your work?

AvH: They read it very differently. It's post their particular sense of the world; it's the colonizer's story.

AC: I ask that partly because you're very interested in claiming freedom for your women, the freedom to move and roam, going boldly where many men have gone before, and aboriginal women must be more confined in their reserves and living spaces, so that motive doesn't seem to come up in their work. And perhaps, like African women, they're more concerned to tell an autobiographical or documentary story first.

AvH: First Nations women in Canada are not necessarily confined to their homes. That was a very nomadic culture.

AC: Originally?

AvH: And in many ways continues to be. There's a lot of movement between the reserves and the cities, and families. But it's a different kind of nomadism. That's why I feel it's not my place to apprehend, because I think there are subtleties that I am probably blind to. I think the best response I've had is to the lead essay in *In Invisible Ink*, where I talk about going across the ice with an Inuit, Pijamini, and we have a whole week together out on the ice as we're travelling between Resolute

Bay and Grise Fiord, and how we begin to communicate, talking about the words for snow and about how his world represents itself. But what I ultimately came to understand and what I said in that essay is that whatever he told me is not something I can reproduce. I'm incapable of it. What I hear is not sufficient for me to act as translator or interpreter. And that I'm not going to put that in an essay. I've worked very hard to grapple with all the different voices that are seeking to articulate their worlds in Canadian literature, and for me, the first generation immigrant kid, I really think my story is anathematic to the story of the First Nations. I'm in many ways responsible for the silencing of theirs. So at a certain stage I feel it's important for me to step back and silence myself so they can get on with their own story.

AC: And not to appropriate their material?

AvH: That's the essay where I'm most satisfied with how I try to share experiences. Although I've written the essay, I cannot write about it. So it is its own contradiction.

AC: But there must be a shared Canadian resonance and sympathy for a lot of things, like your feeling for the north, for example.

AvH: That of course is one of the things that distinguish my writing. For me the north acts as an imaginative lever, and that, I think, is not true for writers who have never gone up there or who choose to ignore its presence.

AC: I read *The Tent Peg* first, and I thought that whole evocation of the north was marvellous, very exciting, especially to a new arrival in Canada,

You often discuss your relation to the reader as an erotic one and writing as a form of anticipatory desire. Are there some problems for feminism in totally eroticizing writing and reading, or is the field always already eroticized? Nancy Miller speaks of the repressed content of fantasy as being an impulse to power rather than eroticism, and you have many scenes in which women triumph over men physically, or exact revenge, equal the score. Is your model of male/female relationships always contestatory?

AvH: The model is one of power, but sexuality is about power. It's about an exertion of power, or a wilful giving up of power. It's all tied in to a complex discourse or dance that we engage in, but it's very much a power struggle. It's just that I don't want it always to be a binary, and so in a sense when my women exact revenge – and they do – they're nasty and mean-spirited and so on. I'm very fond of them for those reasons. But I see it as their being engaged in a labyrinth of the effect of actions as much as it's a righting of some kind of imaginary balance. So it's kind of a vicious circle that we're all hooked into.

AC: You sometimes seem to take your women into vulnerable and threatening situations and then take them out again, in *The Tent Peg*, for instance, and in *No Fixed Address*. I think that's very healthy; it deals with threatening situations for women and shows them escaping.

AvH: I've been accused of empowering women too much.

AC: But can you empower them too much?

AvH: It's the same in *Restlessness*, of course. Here's a woman alone with a man she's hired to kill her.

AC: Yes, that's the most vulnerable situation. But then she arranges that.

AvH: Yes, she arranges it, but nevertheless it can get totally out of control at any moment. She has no idea; that's part of the tension in that novel.

AC: Oh yes, it's wonderfully worked out there. But you're right, the murder scenario is the one which is the most extreme. I was thinking more of forms of sexual oppression, which are handled in the earlier novels. And I think it's a very healthy thing to do, because the reader is then taken through an experience of fear and recovery, of fear and safety.

And that's what many women struggle with, so there the narrative gets into profound psychological terrain.

I had some problems as a reader with the post-structuralist typography in *Places Far from Ellesmere*, though I see how you are trying to de-sentimentalize the "hometown" memory story, and that the work challenges many genre boundaries. What's it like to work and live in a town that you call a "growing graveyard"?

AvH: That has to do with the structure of the city in Calgary, very tall buildings all clustered in one spot. They look like tombstones.

AC: More graveyards than nightclubs?

AvH: But at the same time I think of that description as a positive thing. Graveyards are positive things. In *No Fixed Address* they are places for Arachne to eat her sandwiches. I was born next to a graveyard. I see them as harbingers of human habitation. Of course we're all dust and will crumble, but there's a gentle memory associated with putting up tombstones. So in a strange way, when I'm calling Calgary a growing graveyard, I'm being complimentary. I've taken enormous umbrage at some descriptions. Barry Callaghan said Calgary is nothing but parking lots and prostitutes. I take serious umbrage at that. This is a man who has gone to visit for two weeks and written an article which has been much praised, and he's dismissed the city as being one of temporary exchange. Which is what parking lots and prostitutes are about. For me the graveyard has the notion of place that knows it's going to stay.

AC: I thought that in *No Fixed Address* you used the graveyard in a culturally resonant way, with the old man and the idea of indigenous presence as well as immigration. Almost as if there you were evoking the idea of First Nations and the appropriation of land. I thought there were many echoes there.

But this question was mainly about your attitude to earlier hometown fictions by women. Was *Places Far from Ellesmere* partly a postmodern response to Canadian small town life and the way it was fictionalized earlier in Margaret Laurence's *Manawaka* and Alice Munro's *Jubilee*?

AvH: I think we have a desperate sentimentality about our homes. You can tell that throughout these novels I have an ongoing argument about what home is and where it is and how it exerts its influence on us. In Laurence and Munro there's a need to inscribe these homes, but what comes out is an effusive sentimentality coloured by terrible hatred. Nostalgia will do that to you, I think; there's an edge of dreadful animosity in those things, and yet at the same time they're given a lot of space. I was working with the question: can you write about home without feeling nostalgic or without terrible hatred, for after all home is what we want to escape from even if we know it's the place...

AC: Where everything went wrong?

AvH: Leona Gom says, "Home is the place you go and they have to take you in." So I was working with these notions, and at the same time with the notion of how we are inscribed by home. I think the writer thinks: will I or will I not inscribe my home, but in point of fact each person is already inscribed by home, and to rebound on that text is always a difficult exercise, but one that I think is a challenge. In *Places Far from Ellesmere* the litany that I have of growing up for the character consists of the things she's not supposed to do. So it becomes a place of interdiction. The place where she is presumably freed of her childhood, Edmonton, where she goes to school, becomes a kind of distorted negative experiential space. And Calgary is a growing graveyard because it's full of parking lots and prostitutes.

AC: So Ellesmere is what's left?

AvH: What's left is that you can encounter Anna Karenina, which is in a sense my final argument. For me, home is inside books.

AC: For you home seems to be revising a book.

AvH: Revising, writing, meeting a character again and again that I have met many times. And within the pages of a book is where I find a home, which is most peculiar, but for me it's normal.

AC: For me it's also normal.

AvH: Those six books we carry everywhere in the world with us are our home.

AC: Yes, more nomadology.

Perhaps you could say more about your choice of Anna Karenina as a character to dialogue with and recreate in *Places Far from Ellesmere*. Your "geografictione" does seem to explore links between male authorship, realism, the Canadian north and Russian steppes. Was it because she is the sinful damned woman according to nineteenth century morality? Why is she the figure the heroine moves towards? Was this a kind of rescue operation for a woman badly treated by Tolstoy?

AvH: No, it was a shocking desire for her. And you're right, it's because she's a Russian and comes from St. Petersburg. She lives in the north in Russia, and Russia's north has far more in common with Canada than the southern Balkan area or southern Canada. It was the fact that she was a woman confined by the nineteenth century, and the fact that she was a woman character created by a man, and written very well but then imploded or destroyed. It was the fact, again, that she had committed sexual transgressions. What she does is to have an adulterous affair, which costs her virtually everything.

AC: You could have chosen Madame Bovary for that reason.

AvH: But so much has been written about Madame Bovary, and she doesn't come from the north.

AC: That's true.

AvH: Madame Bovary is not as interestingly realized as Anna Karenina. Because you know what is the source of Anna Karenina's corruption. It is that she reads. So you see she has manifold characteristics for me.

AC: She's a marvellously realized character. One remembers her forever.

AvH: I will forever be grateful to Tolstoy for inventing her.

AC: And she's a sort of double for your protagonist in that she comes from a realistic novel and is embedded in what is your most experimental fiction, or certainly your most experimental to date.

AvH: I would say it is.

AC: So there's a sort of tension there around genre, with the realistic novel, *Anna Karenina*, being a benchmark in realistic fiction.

AvH: One that determined the shape of the realistic novel.

AC: Yes, enormously influential.

Your novels seem to work with and against the homesteading myth, the valorization of life on the land as opposed to the materialism and artificiality of city life. Judith, after a miserable life in the city and an affair with her boss, becomes a successful hog-farmer and seems to be about to settle down with a neighbourly Albertan farmer. The movement in *Judith* is back to the land and a settling into fertility, whereas all your other novels work far more contrapuntally with marriage, domesticity and relationships with men. Also, most of us now live and work in cities: are your isolated settings working within a "wilderness myth" or simply places where gender and other conflicts appear more clearly?

AvH: If you grow up on a farm, again, it's how home inscribes you. You grow up and participate in a narrative whose rituals the urban person really doesn't understand. It's a highly ritualized life, far more influenced by the seasons and the weather and the sunrise than urban-dwellers are. I guess I saw that as a good space for me to lay out the potential discovery and amorphousness of a woman, because farming is an enterprise that requires a lot of energy. And to be financially successful means you have to work really hard.

AC: While I was reading *Judith* I went to the Open University College Royal and saw some piglets and realized what a handful they would be to work with. And you make those practicalities come alive.

AvH: That is, for Judith, her problem: how to deal practically with being a pig-farmer. How to feed them, how to make money out of them so she can buy more feed to produce more so she can feed herself, which is in many ways an elemental problem. Being a secretary, sleeping with your boss, and collecting a presumably adequate pay-cheque nevertheless puts you in a deeply compromised position. In some ways *Judith* is a very simplistic novel, but I really wanted to explore that. The risks that she takes by returning to a rural life are risks that speak to the risks that all women endure but negotiate in many different ways.

AC: And there's a strong female friendship with the farmer's wife. Their conversation brings to life the problems for the farmer's wife, and those of a woman who tries to be a farmer herself. I thought that was very pleasant, and also they're the people who do the agricultural production of the country. That's what a lot of people in Canada actually do.

But I was also asking you about the tension between homesteading and wilderness, or what Heather Murray calls the "pseudo-wilderness" myth that Atwood draws on, or helps to create, in *Surfacing*. Because you also work with rites of passage, and exorcism of damage, and surfacing from the depths, and take your characters through quite sharp challenges.

AvH: The rural experience is also one that I think merits mythologizing. We talk a lot about "the land", the settler experience, the whole notion of civilizing this vast territory, though it is by no means civilized and the territory is still pretty wild. But the rural experience, as a means of making a living by grubbing in the earth, is a very small part of that. Yet the farm, the saga of the family farm, that story is changing very rapidly, especially with the advent of factory farms. You can see it here in southern Ontario. The family farm is dying. It is under siege from every side, and yet for generations it was a sustenance, a mode of life, a ritual with incredible resonance. That was what I was tackling: the very simple story of the family farm. Can it be maintained, and what does it take to engage in that?

AC: Judith doesn't inherit the family farm though. She returns and buys her own piece of land. So it's partly about resisting the passing on of land and patriarchal tradition and finding your own place.

AvH: Yes.

AC: Those scenes in the barn with the pigs are marvellous, such a rich atmosphere. And the novel is very informative because the reader is constantly being shown what it means to be a hog-farmer.

AvH: It's hard work. People say, "Oh, I'd love to have a little farm, and I'd grow this or that." But it's very hard work.

AC: So *Judith* overturns the pastoral myth as well.

The quality of your fiction seems to me to stem from a combination of working-class characters – saleswoman, prospectors, bus-drivers – with literary sophistication in narrative form. Is this class focus something deriving from your own background or a deliberate anti-intellectualism in terms of characters and action? I enjoyed all the humour of situations where your heroine meets writers aand says she's never read a poem in her life, all she wants to do is take the poet to bed.

AvH: That's all poets are good for, right?

AC: I don't know whether farming can be considered working-class, but it's quite a relief to read a novel that's not another Künstlerroman. These are not novels about women who are very close to you in terms of working on creative problems, literary women.

AvH: I must admit I'm very sick of the narcissism of the writer writing about writing. And I understand why. We have limited worlds and experiences, and here we are writing about something we know. We have to make a good job of it. But I do think that class is the one uninflected narrative that we haven't yet figured out how to deal with. We're beginning to work with narratives of race and gender, and we're certainly beginning to work with narratives of sexual orientation, but class cuts across all those. A working-class gay woman is quite different from an academic, middle-class gay woman. They have very different worlds. And the same is true of a working-class First Nations woman and one who works as an administrator or for the government in Ottawa. So for me class becomes the narrative that is most fraught, the most difficult, the one most people would rather not look at, because it's the least visible. We can change class quite easily; we can't change the colour of our skins that easily. So it's a real challenge, because it isn't that I like giving my characters exotic jobs. Making a living is still one of the things that is hardest for people. How do you survive? This is a question of the work we are able to do and how you pay for the groceries. This is the story that we want to elide and forget, yet we live it every day.

AC: I struggle with it all the time.

AvH: We all do. Yet for me this is particularly true of women, because women are inevitably the new poor, especially women who have children, or who have no support structure, or who are old. The narrative of what you are going to do when you are an old woman in this country is a terrible narrative, and I guess it's one I'm always thinking about.

AC: You've also worked at different occupations yourself, so you have varied work experience.

AvH: I worked on the farm a lot as a child. I've been a bush cook, a secretary, a tractor driver, a reader for a blind professor. I've done everything, from the highest intellectual work down to the lowest, shit-digging labour. And that if anything taught me that you cannot take for granted any narratives at all. You only have to dig a ditch for fifteen minutes to know you don't want to do it for the rest of your life. But what if you don't have that choice?

AC: Exactly. Many people don't. But these stories are very informative about labour and the physicality of labour. What does the bus-driver do when she gets to the end of her shift? How does she deal with male passengers who make sexual advances? How much does she earn? I thought that was unusual, that you're taking the ordinary people of the country and showing how their lives are spent on a given, typical day. And also showing what happens to gender codes when jobs normally done by men are performed by women.

AvH: Well, it matters to me.

AC: You wouldn't do it if it didn't matter to you.

AvH: We're passionate about our lives, but I'm not sure we're always passionate about our work. We change domiciles, and partners, and our political positions often, but now we're told that in the course of our lives we're going to have to change our work three or four times, retrain ourselves. And that's the hardest thing. Yet it's what many people are now having to confront. The world of labour is itself changing.

AC: Thank you very much. Would you read a section from "In Visible Ink"?

From "In Visible Ink"

Reader, even invisibled to language, one makes what signs one can. I place my dwarfed foot in the foot-writing left by a polar bear. I circle every iceberg three times, on my right, reading myself a spell. And Pijamini names his world for me: cloud, sun, falling snow, snow on the ground, ice, bear, tracks, caribou, muskox, sundogs, iceberg, seal. He names his family to me, his seven children and their children. He names the points, the promontories, the edges of islands as we pass. I repeat his namings, carefully shaping my mouth and tongue around their inflections and contours, and Pijamini laughs. "Very good, very good. You should come to Grise Fiord, study Inuktitut." He gives me his words, and thus names me, writes my invisible and unlanguaged self into his archeology. I am written, finally, with that nomadic language.

    Reader, reading you, I know you want me to put those words down here, reveal their magic incantation. Never. They are Pijamini's words, not mine, and if I was able to hear them and to mimic them, it was only through his agency. I will not raid them, or repeat them beyond the Arctic sea, beyond the secret worlds of ice. They gave me a reading, read me in that space where I, trying to read anew, was finally written. Reader, this amulet of the first and most final of all crypto-fictions is that one can be disappeared and re-written in a language beyond one's own. Herein resides the ultimate illusion of text: you are not reading me but writing, not me but yourself; you are not reading writing but being read, a live text in a languaging world.

When Words Deny the World: Stephen Henighan

Stephen Henighan, who now teaches Latin American Studies at the University of Guelph, was born in Germany and educated in Canada, the US and the UK. His writing is informed by a detailed world history with a special understanding of Latin America and Eastern Europe as they illuminate their own histories and reflect on Canadian history. He has published widely in both fiction and criticism and has developed a lively and controversial critical view of Canadian literature, as one that ignores or elides both globalization and the social problems within Canada. He is also the Translations Editor at Biblioasis.

Henighan has published three collections of short stories: *Nights in the Yungas* (1992), *North of Tourism* (1999) and *A Grave in the Air* (2007); and several novels: *The Places Where Names Vanish* (1998); *Other Americas* (1990), *Streets of Winter* (2004), *The Path of the Jaguar* (2016) and *Mr Singh Among the Fugitives* (2017). His criticism includes *Assuming the Light: The Parisian Literary Apprenticeship of Miguel Asturias* (1999), *When Words Deny the World: The Reshaping of Canadian Writing* (2002), *Lost Province: Adventures in a Moldovan Family* (2002), *A Report on the Afterlife of Culture* (2008) and *Sandino's Nation: Ernesto Cardenal and Sergio Ramirez Writing Nicaragua, 1940-2012* (2014).

Henighan is especially good at recording the changing relationship between Canada and other communities, which includes South American countries and the immigrant communities within Canada, in their daily struggles to reach an economic and social equilibrium. Young boys growing up in Ontario encounter themselves and a more politically troubled and volatile experience in Latin America, where there have been revolutions instead of a quieter Canadian evolution. His immigrant characters contend with poverty, language and gender codes in an adopted Canada, and in urban centres such as Montreal. His fiction brings an intellectual's questions to Canada in a globalized world of constant change.

Interview with Stephen Henighan

AC: In your first novel, *Other Americas*, you present Canada and Colombia as two marginal countries with various illusions about each other, but the epigraph from V.S. Naipaul argues that Canada is in fact an unconscious compromise with "the West" and that most Canadians live off other people's land without any real awareness. What kind of perspective has being Canadian given you on South American society and politics?

SH: In regard to *Other Americas*, I think that the novel is designed to ask questions rather than to answer them. I think the juxtaposition of the two cultures through the alternating chapter settings – one in Canada, one in Colombia – if it works, brings out certain parallels. Some of these are contrasts, some are similarities, and you do not end up with any direct way of seeing the two cultures as equal, except perhaps in not knowing themselves sufficiently. That is perhaps what I was trying to imply in the epigraph from V.S. Naipaul, which says that Canadians are not self-aware, but also in the epigraph from Jorge Luis Borges, that being Colombian is an act of faith, which implies that at some level you never know exactly where you are and who you are.

I think being Canadian has given me an odd perspective on Latin America, or at least a different one from the Americans, who, although most of them would deny this, have a somewhat imperialist take on Latin America, and from the Europeans, who tend to romanticize it. It's not necessarily more accurate than theirs, but it's different. It draws out different aspects of Latin American society, such as being culturally on the edge or being culturally marginalized. It also struck me when I first went there fifteen or twenty years ago – and I think this is less true today, especially in Mexico or Cuba, both of which have a lot of contact with Canada these days, Cuba through tourism and Mexico through a combination of tourism and business – that people in Latin America knew very little about Canada and weren't even sure where it was, whether it was in Europe or somewhere else. The Spanish language makes it very difficult to explain where Canada is because the expression for the United States is "Norte America", so if you explain that there are two countries in North America and you happen to be from the other one, it doesn't make any sense to them, because it's almost like explaining that the United States is divided into two states. Out of these confusions, perhaps, came my rather offbeat take on Latin America.

AC: Do you think it's a form of modesty and irony that may be inherent in a Canadian outlook? Quite a few commentators suggest that Canada's political role has been that of broker, a middle power's role in the world.

SH: I think that's a fair assessment, and in terms of my experience in Latin America that attitude was inevitable, because if someone doesn't know where your country is located on the map...

AC: You're compelled to be modest?

SH: You can't swagger. You know you're not that important.

AC: I enjoyed very much, in *Other Americas*, the narrative of two boys growing up in Ontario, in what you call a provincial setting, and I liked the way you combined that Bildungsroman with a later story, in which the younger brother conducts a quest to find a basis for political action in the world. There was a gentle critique of stifling Ontario social conventions, and also a partial deconstruction of any easy alliance with a radical peasant revolution. Did the early narrative come out of your own childhood? Was the turn to guerrilla warfare in Latin America a partial answer to the stifling and enclosed world in which the Canadian boys had grown up?

SH: Obviously that's a Latin American answer to a Latin American problem. It was an answer that looked a lot more viable in the early eighties when there were three revolutionary governments in place in Latin America, in Nicaragua, Cuba and Grenada, and two countries, Guatemala and El Salvador, where it looked as though revolutionary governments might soon take power. That answer doesn't look very viable now, and I wouldn't propose it as an answer to Canadian problems, but the treatment of eastern Ontario grows out of my own upbringing, growing up in eastern Ontario as an insider/outsider. By that I mean someone who arrived there as an immigrant but who arrived in the area where there were no other immigrants. So I have a very peculiar experience in terms of Canadian immigrants, at least of my generation and the generation before mine, in that most immigrants have traditionally gone into cities where they've lived in neighbourhoods close to other immigrants from the same countries, but I went to a rural and at that stage very closed Ottawa Valley, where the people I met had intermarried with one another for six generations, so I became deeply assimilated while at the same time being aware that this wasn't really me.

AC: Your family emigrated from Germany?

SH: I was born in Germany, but that's a coincidence. My parents met in the Middle East. My mother is from an upper middle class English background; my father is working class Irish American, born in New York only a few years after his parents had emigrated from Scotland, after an earlier emigration of the previous generation from Ireland. So I wasn't quite sure where I was from, but I knew it wasn't where I was growing up. Yet at the same time I became very much the place where I was growing up, and I think from that may have sprung my need to portray rural Ontario in what I saw as a more dynamic way than, say, Alice Munro, whose work I admire greatly, but who sees Ontario as self-contained. I wanted to see how rural Ontario fitted into the world, and I think that's the origin of *Other Americas*. I was writing that novel in the late eighties when ideas like Free Trade were first being broached, and it struck me that Canadians needed to think about fitting themselves into the western hemisphere in a way that would in my view be more creative and allow for greater flexibility than by simply attaching ourselves to the United States through Free Trade. I wanted an engagement with all of the Americas.

AC: I think that emerges very strongly in your writing. There's a dynamic discussion in your work about ideas of nation.

Do you agree with your character Sonia's analysis of the United States, Canada and Latin America, that it's the American Revolution that made the difference; Spanish America has embraced economic liberalism only, and Canada lives by the Family Compact and the Chateau Clique? What does this last phrase mean? I myself, as an ex-South African, do not believe the dictum, so powerfully enunciated in George Orwell in our time, that all revolutionary ideals necessarily become oppressive.

SH: I don't think there's any suggestion that revolutionary ideals necessarily become oppressive, merely that the liberalism that was revolutionary in the United States in the eighteenth century, because it grew out of the Enlightenment, which was a liberation of all aspects of human behaviour, has been whittled down in our time to a kind of economic liberalism with a bit of hedonism around the edges, which is oppressive for others and arguably for certain classes within the United States as well.

The Chateau Clique was the group that controlled Quebec politics before the advent of Responsible Government in Lower Canada in the middle of the nineteenth century, and they're the analogue in French Canada of the Family Compact in English Canada. I think that view of Canadian society is perhaps a bit outdated. The novel was published in 1990 and has perhaps been a bit surpassed by events such as globalization and Free Trade, which have made the Canadian elite much less powerful and less important than it was previously.

AC: Is your fiction describing the end of an era in Ontario, perhaps in Canada, the end of the family farm and the stable moral codes and conventions? This is something Aritha van Herk deals with from an Albertan perspective in a novel called *Judith*. You have an often comic representation of small town codes for sexuality and marriage, which everyone in your fiction breaks out of, if they're lucky. Were you perhaps breaking out of that perspective yourself, by writing *Other Americas*?

SH: Writing that book was probably part of my breaking out of it, but I have a very divided view of this, because there's a part of me that did grow up in rural Ontario and that remains a Red Tory Loyalist, even though that's not my actual background. I suppose that's one of the oddities of the book, but it's also an oddity of my own upbringing. Having grown up on a farm in eastern Ontario and then spent quite a lot of my formative time in Latin America, I have a kind of Third World Marxism layered over an eastern Ontario Red Tory outlook.

In terms of the end of an era, I didn't realize quite how much the end of an era it was. When I was growing up in the Ottawa Valley, it was popular to cite a statistic that said there were about 20,000 farms in the Ottawa Valley in 1963 and about 10,000 in 1973 and fewer ever since, obviously. It was more that topic that preoccupied me, but of course, with Free Trade and NAFTA and globalization, far more than even I suspected at the time has gone by the wayside in terms of institutions, conventional ways of relating, and old-fashioned social values.

AC: Perhaps I also mean the end of an era in the sense that part of the response to that shifting moral code, which existed in many other countries, of course, was to think that going to places like Latin America and participating in a radical social movement outside your own country was the thing to do. I'm thinking of the romanticism of the sixties and seventies, I suppose.

SH: Yes, it's there in the sixties and seventies, but of course you can trace it farther back to Andre Malraux, Ernest Hemingway, and George Orwell going off to fight the Spanish Civil War from France, the United States and England. A few critics actually commented on the first three stories in my collection, *Nights in the Yungas*, which are set in Nicaragua at the time of the Sandinista government, that they were a bit of a throwback to Hemingway and the Spanish Civil War. The complicating factor for me is that most of those examples are of people going to Spain from societies which they would perceive as being dominant or superior to that of Spain, or at least more modern, to use the language that Malraux would use. But Canada to Colombia is much more complicated, and I think the issues become much more tangled, which may be why it's so interesting to go on writing about them.

AC: You teach language, and both of your novels deal with the relationship between language acquisition and identity. Clearly language learning is one answer to being more than a tourist in a foreign country, but there's also an implication in some of your fiction that proficiency in Spanish can bring some unwelcome or disturbing forms of knowledge of Latin America.

SH: Obviously I've spent quite a lot of my life learning languages, and so a great deal of my early enlightenment came through learning languages, and I suppose that gets translated back into the imaginative worlds I create. Marta, the protagonist of *The Places Where Names Vanish*, begins her life in a society where literacy is minimal. She is literate, and that's quite important, because people who aren't literate have a much harder time learning a second language. So when she comes to Canada she is capable of learning French and also a little bit of English. In Marta's case it seems that language does bring unwelcome knowledge because she imagines while she's living in Ecuador that when she gets to Canada she's going to be living in a pure white gringo heaven, where if money doesn't quite grow on trees she'll be living in quite a comfortable way. She ends up living in an immigrant ghetto in Montreal, having to learn French and English, and discovering that there are extremely complex cultural issues to be found in Canada as well as often many forms of economic hardship. I suppose that's one form of unwelcome knowledge.

AC: The story at the end of *Nights in the Yungas* deals with Quechua as an unwritten language and the site of Inca traditions. Does that story suggest a relationship between sacred traditions and an oral tradition in South America, or perhaps just in Ecuador?

SH: I actually studied Quechua one summer when I was a teenager and at one stage could tumble along in it in a very amateurish way. It's all gone now, but I wanted to bring that in because I thought it was important to recognize that Latin Americans are not all the same, and one of the differences is that they've often come from different linguistic traditions or have different languages lurking in the background of their lives, even if they no longer speak them. Many people in Mexico or Guatemala today are perhaps only one generation away from people whose first language was a native language, and not Spanish. There are other instances of that. People from Chile or Argentina may be only a few generations away from a European immigrant who spoke a different language: Italian, German, or French.

AC: I thought it was a powerful concluding story because it seemed to come from an indigenous perspective, as a way of closing off the earlier dialogues between visitors and Latin Americans in those stories.

Many of your earlier fictions show tourists or visitors to South American countries being shocked into another dimension by sudden experiences, usually of violence. Your first protagonist learns to carry a knife in his sock. Was this part of your experience, or simply a narrative pattern chosen to reveal national differences between peaceful Canadian society and Latin American poverty and struggle? Do I need to carry a knife in my sock if I go to South America?

SH: No, but you may find a knife held at your neck, which is what happened to me. The scene with the protagonist of *Other Americas*, Keith Merrick, being mugged at knife-point, is something that happened to me, but a lot of other things happened to me which I haven't put into the books in direct ways, and they may inform the aura of violence that is there in some of the writing. I had numerous violent encounters: for example, the Caqueta is a region of Colombia that has been under guerrilla control for many years. I was travelling on an overnight bus through there, and an army truck had been blown up. I saw it burning at the side of the road. We were dragged out of the bus in the jungle five times in one night. I've had many experiences of this kind. As recently as five years ago I was strip-searched on the border between

Moldova and Romania. I was also roughed up in the former Soviet Republic by a group of thieves who may or may not also have been policemen. As an over-privileged Westerner, when you go to countries which do not enjoy these privileges, there is a kind of bizarre, perverse and almost sadomasochist transaction taking place, in which you are offering up your body to be pummelled in order for people who are economically oppressed to vent their frustrations, and in turn you may be able to enlarge your own experiences and perceptions. It's an obscene transaction but in a peculiar way almost unavoidable.

AC: "The goal of an artist is to be heard among the people," says one of your characters in *Nights in the Yungas,* yet your characters feel many forms of deracination and often feel isolated among many displacements. *In North of Tourism,* another character says, "I have become an eternal foreigner against my will." How do you perceive your relationship with an audience?

SH: When I began writing, although I'm from the Ottawa Valley originally, my writing career began in Montreal, publishing short stories in literary journals in the eighties, then my first novel, *Other Americas,* in 1990, and my short story collection, *Night in the Yunga*s, in 1992. At that point I was perceived as an Anglo-Quebec writer. My stories appeared in two anthologies of Anglo-Quebec fiction; I was writing a column for the *Montreal Gazette.* I also reviewed occasionally for *The Globe and Mail,* which in the early nineties was much more concerned then than it is now with being Canada's national newspaper, and therefore made a point of having a token Montrealer, Edmontonian, and Vancouverite. When I appeared there I was pointedly described as a Montreal writer. So I started out as an Anglo-Quebec writer, and my books certainly sold best in Ottawa and Montreal, although there was always a small following on the West Coast, largely because of the Latin American subject matter, which appeals more to those on the West Coast than elsewhere.

AC: Because they travel there more often?

SH: Yes, they have more direct contact, partly because they've absorbed the whole Californian obsession with Latin America.

1n 1992 I left Canada, and I spent the next six years in Europe, and my audience pretty well evaporated. Toronto had always been a minimal readership for me, and during the time I was out of the country the Canadian literary world became much more commercially driven. The Canada Council became less important; small presses and literary magazines got into trouble, though many are still going, but they depend more now on special issues and fundraising. The result is – and this is extremely important – that as the Canadian literary world became more commercially driven it also became more Toronto-centric. The two are inextricably linked, though this opinion is not often voiced.

When I came back I found that *The Places Where Names Vanish*, though it attracted some good reviews, had trouble commercially, because I'd lost my Montreal base and had not acquired a base anywhere else in the country, though again there was a ripple of interest on the West Coast.

With *North of Tourism* something strange happened: I seemed to enter the postmodern globalized world. The book sold much better, but I've also discovered that it's become the kind of book read by numerous people quite a bit younger than me, often in their mid-twenties. I've been told by numerous people, and appropriately enough, seen postings on the internet, that say, "I read this book while backpacking around Thailand," or "My friend sent me this book while I was teaching English in South Korea." So I feel as though I no longer have a regional affiliation, and yet it's not possible to be a pan-Canadian writer in the way it was, perhaps, until the mid-1990's. I'm not quite sure where I fit in, but it's probably around the edges, which is not the worst place to be.

AC: I learned a good deal from your fiction about national differences within South America, and within Europe. You occasionally deal with an African heritage in Brazil and link this to female experience of spirit possession and racial denigration in your second novel, *The Places Where Names Vanish*. Is African tradition a hiding place for certain kinds of religious belief, or even political groupings in South America?

How does race figure in social conflicts?

SH: Certainly the African influence in Brazil, and especially in the state of Bahia in northeastern Brazil, is very important, and even many of the words in Bahian Portuguese turn out to be of West African origin. It's true that this is very important in "The Meaning of an End", the first short story in *North of Tourism*, and the African heritage does return in the opening section of *The Places Where Names Vanish*. There I'm dealing with Ecuador, which has a kind of invisible black minority, quite substantial, about 12% of the population, but a black population that's much further away from African traditions than is the case in Brazil. Race is an important source of social division in Latin America. It's not meant to be, but it is. That tension is one I feel I haven't really grappled with as much as I might have done.

AC: It seems to play a part in Marta's sense of being devalued, and part of the tension in her immigration process is her question, "Am I really worthy of this white Quebec society?"

SH: Yes, it is important. Marta perceives it racially rather than culturally because she has very little African culture, and she is half of African ancestry and half of mixed Hispanic and Native ancestry. I think what comes out especially in the Montreal section of *Places* is Marta's grappling with the way in which she transposes her own prejudices, her own false consciousness, if you like, about her racial identity as it would be construed in latin America. She transposes that onto Canadian society, which causes her huge problems, and which I think to some extent she overcomes in order to create a viable life for herself in Montreal.

AC: Those scenes made me think of Erna Brodber's *Myal* and other Caribbean novels, even Jean Rhys's *Wide Sargasso Sea*, where intimations of a spirit world have a lot to do with questions of displacement and with love relationships.

SH: Yes, at the end of *Places*, when Marta is having problems, that unseen world comes back to haunt her, quite literally. It is part of her passage from an animist world to an ultra-materialist world. She has to integrate her animist world into the extremely fast-moving and somewhat intolerant materialistic society of a modern Canadian city.

AC: Many of your narrators or protagonists are women realizing their public commitments, and you deal with gender stereotypes in Ontario, as well as the stifling effects of Puritanism in confronting both heterosexuality and homosexuality. It's quite surprising, because it's Latin American society that is supposed to be so macho and traditional, but you certainly illuminate the constricting effects of constant moralizing and gossip in Ontario society. Is your frequent choice of female protagonists and the representation of homoerotic relationships a deliberate attempt to break down gender binaries?

SH: I think that happened because adopting the female perspective made it easier to develop a dramatic angle on these societies. There's nothing more boring than a heterosexual male, in the sense that the range of possible events is often very limited, especially with a heterosexual male in a stable relationship. I think in searching for stories to tell I found myself drawn to female narrators precisely because they seemed to have interesting stories to tell. Now I see that is partly because they have access to the shifts in identity which, book by book, appear to me to be at the core of my fiction.

As for the uncertainty of sexual identity, in a story like "Blind in Granada" in *North of Tourism*, which is about a character having a crisis in sexual identity, that is a part of the ongoing destabilization of identity that is caused by rapid movement around the globe, erosion of traditional institutions, dispersal of traditional societies and so on. Thus, as other identities become provisional or cease to exert the kind of automatic allegiance that they once did, so sexual identity also becomes somewhat unstable.

AC: In *North of Tourism* you write, "I long to unite the two faces of my soul, the eternal foreigner and the stubborn provincial." I heard echoes of Stephen Dedalus in these words. Is fiction a way of forging an alliance between these two sides of all displaced people? How would you say your perceptions of novelistic technique changed between your two novels, a decade apart, when you shifted from an interwoven narrative to writing from within female peasant experience and shifted the direction of the protagonist's journey, now an immigrant journey toward Montreal? I liked very much the open-ended narrative in *Places*, with a hesitation between two lovers woven into an immigration story, and an ironic ending in that scene between daughter and mother: "Pauvre Maman! Nothing new is going to happen to you again."

SH: Yes, the journey is reversed. *Other Americas* is about Canadians in Latin America, the second about an Ecuadorean woman who emigrates to Canada. The other change is that the intercalated chapters of the first novel give way to a much more linear narrative. The reason for that came directly out of my own rather ornery reaction to some of the things happening in Canadian writing in the mid and late nineties, as I was finishing *Places*. I found that as we got swept away by NAFTA and globalization it was very difficult to find Canadian novels that drew a bead in any coherent way on Canadian life and society. Canadian novels were either set in remote times, were vague historical fictions, or were set in a romanticized Maritime region, with a welter of metaphor which might or might not translate into anything concrete: Ondaatje's *English Patient* and Anne Michaels' *Fugitive Pieces* are two salient examples.

I disliked this because I saw it as colluding in concealing much of what was happening in Canada as a result of Free Trade, NAFTA and globalization. I felt that a lot of the misery in the street wasn't being allowed into the fiction, because the fiction had become too rarefied, not in a literary sense, but in appealing to an elite who didn't want to see things presented too clearly because it would make them uncomfortable. Portraying the misery in the street might have forced the bourgeoisie to face its collaboration with what was happening to the country. I thought that was where many beautiful shimmering metaphors in Michaels and Ondaatje's fiction were coming from.

In the last few drafts of *Places* I made a deliberate attempt to make the language as hard and as uncompromising as possible. A few people said there were too many active, aggressive verbs in it, but I did make a very deliberate effort to pare down the language, to use active verbs, and to focus very closely on the details of daily life for people in some situation of deprivation, to the point of including the price of a piece of bread left over at the bakery, the day-after leftovers. This was really my reaction to what I read as a kind of mushy evasiveness in a lot of Canadian fiction at the time.

AC: An evasiveness about immigrant realities and economic hardship?

SH: Yes, about general Canadian social realities in the conditions of the nineties. I thought much of the fiction was running helter-skelter in the opposite direction. I wanted, within a fictional frame, to throw this in the reader's face. So that is what I did.

AC: Have you read Ondaatje's *Anil's Ghost*?

SH: No, not yet.

AC: That also deals with political realities in another country, Sri Lanka.

SH: I gather the language is rather less metaphorical.

AC: It's extremely technical, dealing with forensic medicine and archeology. Ondaatje has never dealt much with the political realities of ordinary people in Sri Lanka. There was only the family memoir, *Running in the Family*.

SH: There's a little bit of politics in *Running in the Family*, but not much.

AC: There's often a tension in your work between private and public commitments, especially well worked out, I thought, in the concluding story of *North of Tourism*, "The Alliance of Tiny Kingdoms", where the history of Europe during World War II becomes a coda for, or response to the broader tension between different Americas in your other work. That story ends with a powerful vision of foot soldiers and faith, which captured, for me, the sense that revolutions and wars happen in ordinary time, something I've been thinking about in relation to South Africa, now in its tenth year from the release of political prisoners and the unbanning of political opposition groups. What is the context of that concluding story in *North of Tourism*?

SH: As you point out, it's the first time I've written a historical piece. It's a long short story, and it's set during World War I. The history of that period is much as it's written there. The Republic of Montenegro is one part of former Yugoslavia that was never conquered by the Ottoman Empire (Croatia and Slovenia were others). It retained a kind of purity, whereas much of the rest of the peninsula became hybridized, and I thought this was a fascinating thing to explore.

Montenegro was destroyed as a country, wiped off the face of the map during that war and was later integrated into Serbia. At a later stage Marshal Tito restored it as an independent republic, largely as a way of fragmenting Serbia and breaking down Serbian dominance within Yugoslavia, because the problem Tito had to deal with in his ethnic balancing act was that there were so many more Serbs than anyone else.

That story is an attempt to grapple with the dissolution of the nation-state in our time, and it portrays that nation-state as something both cherished and yet suffocating. It has a purity that is part of its definition as a nation-state, but, as you say, a large dose of belief is important, because after all Montenegrins are nearly Serbian. They speak Serbian; they simply have a slightly different accent. They're different mainly because they believe they're different, and, of course, sewn into the story are numerous parallels with Canadian history, so that the relationship between Montenegro and Serbia becomes a kind of allegory of the relationship between Canada and the United States.

AC: And of Quebec within Canada?

SH: No. The parallel with North American relationships is something which a couple of Canadian reviewers embraced with open arms and were very excited about. I discovered, however, that both American and Serbian readers find the novella rather offensive.

AC: There's no pleasing people.

SH: No. Neither of them likes the analogy. There's only one place where I've consciously diverged from history in that novella. Montenegro was wiped off the map in 1916 when the Serbian forces had to retreat before the advancing Austrians. Austria took over Montenegro for a few years and was driven out by the Serbs who integrated Montenegro into Serbia until Tito slashed it off again. The one thing I've changed is that the retreating Serbian forces didn't actually pass through Cetinge, the capital of Montenegro. They actually travelled further south. For dramatic reasons I had to make them veer north.

AC: I liked very much that portrait of an exhausted soldiery. It said so much about the war, and also victory, and who pays the price of war on a daily level.

How does teaching at the University of Guelph answer the need to love "the local custom and the cosmopolitan blend" that you describe in *North of Tourism*?

SH: I'm very lucky in that I have a department which has allowed me mornings free to write and has scheduled all my classes in the afternoon. That enables me to keep going. I have a book of essays, *When Words Deny the World*, coming out with Porcupine's Quill. And I've just about completed a new collection of short stories somewhat resembling *North of Tourism*, also about displacement, but this time focussing much more on the influence of history, beginning and ending with World War II. So there's more historical writing. There are a couple of novels floating around in the background, but I'm not sure when they'll be finished.

Journalism does keep me in touch with things, though it's a bit of a burden to do the journalism on top of creative writing, and also the academic writing I need to do in order to maintain my status as a viable academic. I like to do a bit of journalism and also reviewing, because it forces you to read things you might not otherwise read, and it propels you into contemporary debates in a way that I think helps the fiction, though it may not be apparent at the time.

AC: Thank you. Would you read the concluding section of "The Alliance of Tiny Kingdoms" In North of Tourism?"

From "The Alliance of Tiny Kingdoms"

Preoccupied by my thoughts, I miss the ripple of motion swinging down the line. Even the skeletal horses have lifted their muzzles. The French cultural attaché shakes my shoulder. The Serbian officers are smiling. "What is it?" I ask, like a creature emerging from hibernation.

"The men at the front of the line have reached the lip of the mountains," a Serbian officer reports in French. "They can see the coastline below. There is no snow at sea level. The British and French fleets are moored there waiting for us. We didn't believe they would actually come to evacuate us."

I will live to see my daughter! I shout and leap. The Italians join me. Even the weary French ambassador emits a solemn, "Bravo, mes amis!"

Then we fall silent, embarrassed by our childish jubilation. The cadaverous men around us, plagued by wounds, hunger, illness, the loss of homes and families, the death of comrades, stumble forward. As we approach the brink of the mountains, the incredible drop – jagged and barren at first, then scraggy brown, then pliant green – careers away below us. The distant, wavering coastline breaks into a broad hook in whose lee shelter the grey trinkets of the two navies.

Around me, muffled figures drop to their knees, exposing gnarled heels visible through rents in the rags swaddling their feet. They mutter words that sound like an incantation. A few of them, unable to sustain their prayers, break into sobs. They cough and choke as tears crawl down their faces.

Glancing around, I realize that many of the soldiers have remained on their feet. "Why have only some of them got down on their knees?" I ask the French-speaking officer.

He looks away from the view of the fleet, seeming to notice the kneeling men for the first time. "Those ones," he says, "must be the Montenegrins."

The Irish Descendants: Jane Urquhart

Jane Urquhart was born in Northern Ontario and spent her childhood in Toronto. She is a 1971 graduate of the University of Guelph's English program. Urquhart has been a writer in residence, a creative writing teacher and a lecturer at several Canadian universities.

Her poetry collections include *I'm Walking in the Garden of His Imaginary Palace* (1982), *False Shuffles* (1982), *The Little Flowers of Madame Montespan* (1984) and *Some Other Garden* (2000). She has also published a number of novels: *The Whirlpool* (1986), *Changing Heaven* (1990), *Away* (1993), *The Underpainter* (1997), *The Stone Carvers* (2001), *A Map of Glass* (2005), *Sanctuary Line* (2010) and *The Night Stages* (2015). Her short stories were collected in *Storm Glass* (1987).

The Whirlpool was the first Canadian novel to win France's prestigious Prix du Meilleur Livre Étranger. *Changing Heaven* appeared in 1993. *Away* won a Dublin Literary Prize and the Ontario Trillium Award. Her fourth novel, *The Underpainter*, won the 1997 Governor-General's Award for Fiction.

In Urquhart's fictions Celtic worlds and literary traditions are imaginatively refashioned to explore the nature of artistic truth and its relevance to women's quests for psychic wholeness. She also conjures up the lives of earlier writers, characters, and Canadian settlers to evoke the literary and cultural background of a modern multicultural Canada.

Jane Urquhart Interview

AC: In *The Little Flowers of Madame de Montespan* you chose to write poems on a place and historical setting far from Canadian realities, and in a restrained cool style far from the laid-back colloquial style or postmodern playfulness of many Canadian poets. Did you choose your subject or did it choose you? And is the collection a meditation on the waning power of a king's mistresses, or on the waning power of kingship itself?

JU: First of all, to confront the physical context, I was in France for a year with my husband, who was on sabbatical. He is a visual artist and was doing a lot of drawing in France. I had a very young child at that point, which meant I was constrained in a few ways. I would go with my husband to places like Versailles, and he would draw. I would be left with Emily, my daughter. I spent a lot of time in the gardens of Versailles as a result of Tony's doing a number of drawings of that garden. He does very detailed drawings so it took quite a time.

While I was there I became very interested in this kind of landscape, which was so controlled. And I think, when you mention that the style of that book is very restrained and controlled, I think that the style reflected that landscape, or the place that I was writing about determined the style. What interested me about this control of landscape was the power that was behind it. I knew this place was about power. I could tell even before I knew the details. Obviously I knew the kind of general knowledge details about Louis XIV, but I hadn't been able to research him and his life, and his women, until much later, but I knew, just being in those gardens, that they were designed to make one feel that there was a powerful male presence that was in control of all that landscape, which went in all directions. You can, in fact, be in the middle of the garden and still be able to see the palace; there are different territories associated with it.

So I began to wonder what it would be like to be involved with a man like that, and that's how I came across Madame de Montespan, who was Louis XIV's second mistress, his first having been shipped off to a convent by him, and his last having been Madame de Montesquieu, who really controlled the king. He went through three stages; in the last the mistress was in control of the king instead of the other way around. Madame de Montespan really interested me because she tried to poison him. One of the ways she tried to poison him really caught my attention. Instead of poisoning his food, she sprinkled arsenic powder inside one of his silk shirts. Apparently it can be ingested through the pores; she wasn't the first to try this. That was the end of the relationship, you'll be surprised to hear.

However, while I didn't want to think about this too consciously, I realized I was writing about something larger than the specifics of the relationship. I was at this point living a pretty narrow life. A wonderful life, I wasn't unhappy, but I wasn't worldly in the sense of understanding the larger political events going on all around me, although they were affecting me nevertheless. This is a story, from the point of view of Madame de Montespan, of a quest for freedom, a kind of coming to grips with the animus, how the animus can respond, sometimes with much confusion, to the feminine. It was a very interesting experience that involved a huge amount of research. And that's interesting, too, because it is distilled into this tiny little book. It was a really important book for me.

AC: Your take on power and worldliness, would you say this was a Canadian response to Europe?

JU: It may have been. That's very true, that the subject matter really did choose me. Again, I wasn't too conscious of what I was doing. In retrospect, yes, I had never experienced that kind of landscape before. And also there's a poem in there, quite a light poem, but it's called "The King's Nightmare", and the poem is about Louis XIV having a nightmare that relates to Niagara Falls. The French called Canada "terre sauvage", wild country, and the king has a nightmare in which he's in a landscape he can't control, and that landscape is Canada.

AC: Then it circles back to the idea of a French presence in Canada as well. That's significant given the work you did later in your fiction on the Niagara region.

You sometimes speak of writing as escape, as play, and your fiction seems to aim at creating a self-sufficient alternative world rather than an approximation to contemporary Canadian realities. Does your writing spring from a sense that Canadian realities at the time you began writing were perhaps too dull or banal for your purposes, not suitable material for fiction?

JU: No, I should say, while a lot of my work is set in Europe, and I've spent a lot of my time in Europe, some of my books really do have to do with things that are "Canadian" – the Canada I grew up in, a looking back, I suppose, rather than dealing with contemporary issues, or looking forward.

AC: When we talk of "escape" or "play", it's not then an escape in the sense of wanting to get away from the Canadian realities that surround you? Some writers have said that Canada was dull or a place to escape from. There's a sense that the literary tradition you invoke is British; you often work through nineteenth century literature and literary figures such as the Brontës and Browning. Did you grow up with a sense that Canada was not easily written about directly because it was not the stuff of literature? Literature was something that happened in England?

JU: I certainly grew up with the knowledge that literature was something that happens in England, and then, as I grew older, literature was something that happens in England and the United States. But having said that, I was always fascinated by Canadian subject matter and I never really found it boring, but then my family background is perhaps unusual, though in Canada everybody's family background is unusual. We're all immigrants unless we're First Nations people. And I came from an Irish background, which means I have a long history of eccentricities and stories. I've always been fascinated by the connections between landscape and story, and therefore I have a hard time understanding the idea of Canada as dull.

AC: I ask this question because you've discussed fiction as a "journey away from reality". I wondered if there was a deliberate decision not to reflect the Canadian social or political world. When I started reading your fiction, *The Whirlpool* and *Changing Heaven*, many of the characters and situations seemed to be screened through British literature and the nineteenth century.

JU: Earlier in my life I think I did believe that Canadian life was not the stuff of literature. When we studied English, we were studying British literature, not Canadian. I remember, for instance, here at the University of Guelph there was one course, a one-term course, in Canadian literature taught by Elizabeth Waterson. It was a wonderful course, but it wasn't enough for me, and I believe the texts discussed came to a halt somewhere around 1950. It was a survey course. And in high school, public school, there was no mention of Canadian literature except for the Confederation poets, and Bliss Carman, Archibald Lampman, people of that era.

But I think that the real reason that I was working through a European screen is because I was spending so much time in Europe, and yes, it did seem other to me, more magical and appealing, but at the same time I think the fact that I was in Canada made me look back toward Canada. Canada became "other" as well, and became more magical. I became very interested in the kinds of things that had happened in the Canadian past.

One of the magical things about Canadian subject matter, especially historical subject matter, is that it's so fresh. When you're researching someone like Darcy McGee, who figured in *Away*, my third novel, you're doing primary research. You're getting your hands on the papers because there's not much on him, though two or three books have been written. He's a hugely interesting figure, an Irish-Canadian poet, and quite well known in Ireland. Our approach to our own history is so vague and uncertain that no one has really managed to draw it all together, and that, for me, is tremendously exciting.

AC: The research field was wide open, and you would often take off from research?

JU: Oh yes. Each book is born in a different way. When I mention that *Away* is an Irish-Canadian story set mostly in the nineteenth century, I had decided to write a book very vaguely based on my own family history, and from there I moved into things Irish-Canadian. We hadn't studied that. The small amount of Canadian history we'd learned was the history of the French and the English. It never occurred to them to tell us about the Irish. None of the troubles that the Irish left Ireland with disappeared when they came to Canada. It's a quite violent and vibrant history.

AC: In an early short story sequence, "Five Wheelchairs", you seem to use the wheelchair image as a suggestion that people perhaps create their own limitations and obsessions, and in the final one there's an art teacher who suddenly sees that his pupil has painted a wonderful turbulent reality that he himself has chosen to ignore. This drawing master seems to be a forerunner of the painter Austin in *The Underpainter,* who suffers from emotional frigidity. Did painting, in that novel, offer you a model for what literature also has to leave out, or chooses to leave out?

JU: Those stories were the very first short stories that I wrote, when I had decided to move from verse to prose. Again, I'm not quite sure where they came from, or why, except that once again they're connected to my husband Tony's work. He's definitely not the model for these unpleasant visual artists I create.

AC: I wasn't thinking that he was.

JU: I felt I should say that, because a lot of people do think so, people who don't know him. In the same way that he had been drawing in the gardens at Versailles when I began my poems, he had been doing this series of drawings of a strange old Victorian wheelchair, and also a series of confessionals. This was also during the year we were in France, which was an incredibly productive year for me, partly because I'm not particularly bilingual, and that meant I was kind of bottled up; I wasn't able to go out and talk. So I probably wrote more during that year than I have ever since.

AC: Are those his drawings in the story sequence?

JU: Those are his drawings. I thought, Tony's done five drawings of wheelchairs, perhaps I should write a story for each of those wheelchairs. Tony's done a series of seven confessionals, one for each of the seven deadly sins – that was complete coincidence – then I wrote the seven confessionals as well. I think this has happened more than once with my short stories, that they were a kind of rehearsal for longer fiction, because at that stage I didn't believe that I could in fact write a novel. I felt that the form was too large for me. I didn't have the confidence to approach it, and I was pretty amazed that I could finish a short story at that stage. I found later, for instance, that my story called "John's Cottage", which is also in that collection, *Storm Glass*, is almost like an outline for my novel *Changing Heaven*. Or at least one side of that novel, because it's also about a balloonist from Yorkshire and various other things. But the young woman in that story is probably the young woman who appears in *Changing Heaven*.

AC: That explains why the stories in "Five Wheelchairs" read very much like modernist, imagist stories. I can see them as a transition from poetry to longer pieces of prose. Do you see what I mean about the painter figure as a kind of model for Austin in *The Underpainter*, the artist, though I suppose he's more of an art-teacher than a painter? But then part of the point is that contrast between the two functions: the teacher and the artist.

JU: Also, now that you've raised this topic, it's difficult to see one's own work in terms of recurring themes, but the whole idea of restraint, and that being part of the masculine character, seems to happen over and over. I'm very fascinated by that; I can't seem to get it out of my system, in the sense that I want to explore it again and again. In fact, it's a topic in the book I'm working on now. But certainly Louis XIV and the restrained garden, and the drawing master you refer to, and then of course Austin Fraser in *The Underpainter* are similar figures. And in fact there's an art historian in *Changing Heaven* who has the same kind of character. It must be a side of myself.

AC: It probably is, but I think it's also that your work seems to keep exploring the boundary between spontaneity and control, points at which things are inclined to burst free. And art's way of ordering that, and maybe for women it's quite important that it should be ordered.

JU: Maybe.

AC: The following quote from Ann in *Changing Heaven* seems to sum up many things: "It was as though her life were being lived, uncomfortably and secretively, inside the great dark, rattling carriages of nineteenth century fiction." Much of your work is filtered through the nineteenth century, especially the Romantic and Victorian writers: Browning, Shelley, and the Brontës. You show the Romantics and Victorians turning from private into public figures and sometimes being fated to live out their own myths. Could you talk about the causes and the motives for this choice of nineteenth century literature as a vehicle for your vision, especially in *The Whirlpool* and *Changing Heaven*?

JU: I imagine the real motivation was that I was a compulsive reader as a child, and I read mostly great big thick Victorian novels, and I did find them hugely interesting. Much like the child in *Changing Heaven*, I read *Wuthering Heights* at an early age, and then I read it over and over again. By brothers were quite a lot older than I was, so I had a lot of time to myself, and most of it was spent trying to make sense of *Ivanhoe* and books like that.

It seemed to me that the Brontës were really writing their books for children. I still think that both *Jane Eyre* and *Wuthering Heights* are children's books. They begin when the protagonist is a child; childhood is a major part of the structure of the books. By the time Catherine and Heathcliff have grown up, you're so sewn into the text as a child that you really are still interested despite the fact that the book has now moved into adult territory. And I spent a lot of time playing Jane Eyre, playing Heathcliff and Catherine, and trying to encourage other children to play these things with me. These children looked at me as if I was insane, which I may well have been.

I don't think I ever lost my fascination with that world, and of course I grew up in a family that had not changed much since the nineteenth century. My father and mother lived in the city of Toronto, but my extended family, where we spent all our weekends and summers, lived in nineteenth century farmhouses with split-rail fences and woodstoves in the kitchen, and draft horses in the fields, all of that. That world, Canada – at least small-town Ontario – had been patterned on the nineteenth century, had been settled in the nineteenth century, the concession roads laid out in the nineteenth century, and until twenty years ago that world still remained intact, and you can still see bits and pieces of it.

AC: When you turned to that reading, you were also turning to your own childhood, that settled, stable word you grew up in?

JU: Yes and no. In terms of time period, yes, but in terms of surroundings, no, of course, because I didn't live in Haworth. When I went to Haworth for the first time I was just delighted because, unlike Canada, that part of Yorkshire hasn't changed. A Canadian expects to find any sort of landmark built upon, condominiums everywhere, no sense of the past at all, yet there in Haworth the past was still intact.

AC: Were you interested in reanimating history? You seem to have a wonderful talent for making history come alive through certain personages and landscapes.

JU: I think for me, because reading is such an intense experience, those figures were already animated. All I needed to do was record what they were doing. Reading is intensely visual for me; I'm definitely not in the room I'm in. I'm in a room I've created in my mind, an inner theatre, as I call it, where these things are taking place. That started to happen when I was a child, and there was always more to the environment I had entered imaginatively than there was in the text. I would be seeing what the weather was like outside the windows, and if there was a vase of flowers in the room, all kinds of things that weren't necessarily in the text. So it was easy for me to then take the step beyond that, and take what I had managed to imagine around a text and create some of those fictions.

AC: Emily Brontë's ghost says that "all love affairs are pure fiction" and that people in it usually imagine quite different love affairs. Many of your women, those who are not ghosts, are constrained either by unimaginative men, or by social conventions and decorum, or, like Arianna, by men who are their obsessed managers, or, like Sara in *The Underpainter*, men who exploit them twice over, as models and as women. At the end of your story, "Italian Postcards", there is a woman, Clara, who is linked to a saint, Santa Chiara, by the intensity of her emotional pain, by heartbreak. Though your work is not obviously feminist, I took it to be feminist in that you repeatedly show, especially in portrayals of the nineteenth century, the extent to which men are identified with social order, language and authority, while women ceaselessly spin words in order to create a space for themselves, for survival. Would you agree?

JU: I fully agree with that. I can remember when I knew that I was going to be a writer. It was a pretty dramatic moment. When I was first married to my husband, he had custody of the children from a previous family, so that I had custody of his children. They were marvellous kids, and we had a good time, and then I had a baby. This meant that I was very domestically challenged, shall we say. There was a lot of housework. I remember everyone had left the house, all the breakfast dishes were there, and the kitchen was a mess. The baby was crying, the porridge was on the floor, and all of a sudden I thought, "I'm going to be a writer." That was when I knew, and I haven't stopped since. That was over twenty years ago. That baby is now twenty-two years old, and she was six months then.

I remember I pushed the dishes on the kitchen table aside and sat down and began to write. It was so clear to me, and yet I hadn't felt constrained. I hadn't felt particularly unhappy. It wasn't as if I was searching for a way to break out, but I did have to break out. And I'm sure that's partly why those kinds of things crop up again and again in my work. It's fascinating to me that there's such a difference between the careers of men and women in the literary world. That's pretty superficial, and easy to see.

AC: I don't think it's discussed that often, not in Canada, at any rate.

JU: Maybe not. After I published *The Underpainter*, an awful lot of men, and a lot of women, would almost say to me: What was a nice girl like you doing in a mind like that? How could you? Why did you create thus unpleasant character? And I would say, well, what exactly did he do that's so unusual? He didn't rape anyone, or kill anyone. He just abandoned people.

AC: And arranged the world on his own terms.

JU: Somehow I don't think that's all that unusual, but people were quite shocked, and I realized within two or three months of these questions coming at me during interviews that it was because I was a woman. Had Mordecai Richler created that character, first of all, the character would not have seemed nearly so offensive as he clearly did to many people, and secondly, no one would have been surprised. But because he came from me, it was very shocking to a number of people. There's a gender difference right there. Just the fact of being a woman changes the collective attitude to your work. You can certainly understand why women would publish under male pseudonyms in the nineteenth century when things were that much worse. I've probably been writing about this more unconsciously than consciously, but that's not to say that I'm not conscious of it.

AC: I think perhaps your style is so restrained that the protest is not very evident. The protest is there, but it's contained within a cool style.

JU: Part of the reason for that is that I'm not interested in creating a tract. My primary motivation in writing fiction is to create fiction, not to make a political statement. I think that often it works more powerfully that way.

AC: At the heart of *The Underpainter* you have a few little lost girl figures, almost autistic figures, who seem to be the kernel of that rather deprived female figure who comes up in various guises in the novels.

JU: I should tell you that the little lost Jane Eyre figure is based upon an absolutely true story. The girl's name really was Jane Eyre. I would never have the nerve to be that outrageous. There was a little girl lost in the woods near Coburg, which is the place that Davenport is based on, in the early nineteenth century, and her name was Jane Eyre. I read a newspaper account, an old newspaper, as part of primary research, and I thought, how fascinating.

AC: I wanted to ask you about responses to landscape. The Niagara Falls region in *The Whirlpool* seemed to draw together the restrictive side of Ontario society, small town convention, and its potential for romantic adventure, ruggedness and waterfalls. What did this landscape mean to you while you were writing the book?

JU: Part of what drew me to that landscape was another book. Because I operate so unconsciously I often don't realize what is motivating me until I've finished the book, but two or three years after I'd finished I realized, of course, that whole business of the various stages of the river seemed to me to echo another book I was fascinated by as an adolescent, *Paterson* by William Carlos Williams. It's divided into sections: the river above the falls, the river below the falls, and it's a long poem, not a piece of prose.

I remember being very excited about it when I was fourteen or fifteen, because I didn't quite understand it, and that made it even more magical. That's why poetry was very resonant for me as an adolescent:

some part of me did understand it, but an awful lot of me didn't, and that was a perfect combination. So I would read it, and reread it. I suppose they were like sacred texts; you had to be involved in an act of interpretation the whole time you were studying it. And one of those texts was *Paterson* by William Carlos Williams.

But I was also again interested in Canadian history, whether it gets saved or lost. What makes a border? Why does it matter? Because Niagara Falls is now one of the ugliest places on earth. You can sit there and your view is of the USA. It's just across the river. What is it that makes the place across the river so different from us? Also, my mother, who is a great ranter, spent long periods of my childhood saying, "Those Americans, they think they won the War of 1812. Well, they didn't." The figure of the military historian is partly based on my mother on the one hand, and on a real military historian on the other.

AC: You seem to contrast male ways of knowing, or doing history, with female ways. I'm thinking of Munro's rural historian, in *Lives of Girls and Women*, who wants to chart the whole of southern Ontario and get all of the facts, roads and holdings down on paper, objectively, and then there's this different response, wanting to do something completely different from or as well as getting the facts straight. I loved the whole world of the museum, the "floaters", a world of death but transmuted by water. That macabre collection of objects, like George's collection of porcelain in *The Underpainter*. In a crisis these collections get exploded, when the characters break free.

JU: The figure of the undertaker's widow was based on my husband's grandmother, who really did run the oldest funeral home in Canada, which was in Niagara Falls. I found her notebook, and it was called "The Little Floater Book". I never met her, but just the idea of doing that fired up my imagination. The whole idea of writing a novel came from that. I just knew when I found that book that I would have to write a novel.

AC: *Changing Heaven* has a lot to do with haunting, ghosts, "solitary women of words" like the Brontës, conversations between revenants, and a woman who used to perform in the ether, a balloonist, Arianna. Would you talk about your ghosts? Those conversations seemed to give you such freedom.

JU: I went to live in Yorkshire for a while. I was obsessed by the Brontës and had to go there, and my daughter's name is Emily; she went to school in Stanbury, which is Gimmerton in *Wuthering Heights*. While I was there I discovered a tombstone with a balloon on it, and asked around, and got the local story, and heard that a woman had parachuted out of a balloon during a town fair. The parachute hadn't opened, and she died. When I heard the story, I thought, if you had died on those moors, you'd undoubtedly run into Emily Bronte's ghost. Then you'd be out there with her, and you'd have great fun. That was what the book was for.

AC: I got interested in your treatment of male rescuers. Ann, the protagonist, suffers from a love affair with an unimaginative Canadian. When I got to the end of *The Underpainter*, I was frustrated that there was no happy ending. I wanted one, at least.

JU: No, no happy endings.

AC: There is a rescuing Yorkshireman at the end of *Changing Heaven*.

JU: Yes, *Changing Heaven* does have a happy ending.

AC: Yes, but my question is, are you depicting women who want too much from love and whose fantasies do some damage? Brontë's romantic heroes have persuaded us all that there's a Rochester or Heathcliff waiting for every single woman, especially in the north of England?

JU: I think a lot of women are excited by the idea of Heathcliff, and the more miserable the man the more attractive he is. The bad tempered Byronic hero who stomps around in a great temper tantrum most of his life has been made into a very romantic figure as a result of the Brontë books. But I also think it's because of the many spin-offs from the Brontë books, a kind of mutation of them that has really caused the damage.

The reason I chose John as a rescuer had less to do with his gender, and more to do with his social status. I was very interested in that sense of contentment that springs from knowing where your place is. I don't necessarily mean that in a socially hierarchical sense, but knowing that you are of this landscape. I was very moved by the people in Yorkshire in that, for instance, people who'd worked in cotton or woollen mills as children were not unhappy about that. When you asked them about childhood, they wouldn't say, "Was I ever exploited as a child. Where's the government reparation?" They remembered happy times, going off on Sunday School picnics with other children. There was a kind of pride: "That mill down there was where I worked as a girl."

I was very impressed by the people and interested to discover that they were such opposites to the academic figure of the art historian, for instance. While I was in Stanbury, I would be in the pub on Friday nights, and older people whose grandparents had been Patrick Brontë's parishioners were telling me stories that their grandparents had told them, about the Brontë girls, and what they were like, and why they thought they were like that. And meanwhile, over there at Haworth, you would see a lineup of dogged Brontë scholars going into the library, going through the same material over and over when it was in fact so alive. And so I suppose John was more of life; he was life; he was alive.

AC: And then that's a side of the Brontës, too, that sense of being rooted in that area, if you think of the other Bronte novels, of *Shirley*, the whole exploration and knowledge of industry in that area. In a way it also undercuts romantic stereotypes. It's the solidity of knowing a particular place very well, a particular geography.

JU: And what story comes from that, how narrative comes from that because of oral tradition.

AC: Isn't it amazing how long stories can last, over generations, and you often get your freshest details that way.

JU: One old woman said to me about the Bronte sisters, that her grandmother had said, that the problem was that, "Shoes wouldn't, and clogs doesn't." That meant that the men who wore shoes wouldn't have anything to do with the minister's daughters, and the men who wore clogs, the working class, dared not have anything to do with the minister's daughters. I thought, what an incredible saying. Sums it up. Otherwise they would have married and had twenty-seven children and never written any books.

AC: In *Away* you deal with Irish heritage, and legend. I was very interested in your statement that the legend of people being stolen "away" is a metaphor for immigration, and the accompanying loss of self or identity. I suppose in this case the woman who is marked by this experience, by life, could stand for the whole body of Irish immigrant experience in Canada. Is that how you intended it to work? It's a very rich metaphor.

JU: Yes, it's a rich and multi-dimensional metaphor, but in terms of immigration I think it was quite conscious. I increasingly found during that period of my life, which wasn't that long ago, that many of my friends come from somewhere else, originally. They'd become Canadian, or landed immigrants, but they had grown up sometimes in another culture, sometimes just in another place. As a result I began to question, as a multi-generational Canadian, what it had been like for my own ancestors to leave behind a complete culture and family, take this hideous ocean voyage, and come to this freezing cold country. And I also began to wonder what had been left behind, and what had come with them, and there was no real way, apart from a kind of atmosphere around my family, for me to determine that.

I mean, although there were stories, they were all stories set in Canada. They rarely talked about anything that had happened in Ireland, and yet Ireland had become this unbelievably wonderful, idealized, perfect emerald green island, that none of them had ever seen, of course, in which people were being unjustly oppressed by a vicious mother country.

I found all of that very fascinating. I thought that one of the few things that actually bound us all together, at a time when Canada was rapidly changing, was the fact that, whatever generation it happened in, we had all come from somewhere else. Someone in our past had undergone this feeling of being split, a sense that reality was somewhere else, and that had entered the spirit of my family. They still thought the old world was the best world. Heaven will be in Ireland. They'd weep when they heard Irish songs. That mythology had come with them.

AC: Was *Away* a narrative that meant a coming into your Canadian heritage for you? Because it does seem to me that *The Underpainter* is more about Canadian history and society than your earlier books. Did the writing of *Away* make a big difference?

JU: Yes, *Away* was really a kind of homecoming. I wrote a lot of things that were a lot closer to me than I ever had written about before, even in terms of place, for instance. Loughbreeze Beach is a place where there is an old family house, that's been there for a long time. It wasn't floated down the lake to get there, but it's been there for many years. And there were characters in that book who were actually based on people I know who have Irish connections. I had a lot of fun with that. Thomas J. Doherty who is in the book – the book is partly dedicated to him – was an Irish Canadian I knew who lived out in the country near my family, very eccentric. It was a kind of gift to my family, although I made it up. It was great fun to write.

AC: In *The Underpainter* you deal more directly with Canadian history in the period of World War I, and I wondered if your painter, Austin, was intended to represent some of the necessary detachment artists must feel during wartime. There seemed to be an important debate running through the novel concerning war and art. Does Austin also represent capitalism? There seemed to be a kind of national allegory there, because he has the shares in the silver mines, whereas Sarah is the one who has a living link with the mine through her father. How important is it that Austin is American?

JU: I think it's an issue, but I don't think it's a major issue. From what

I remember, when I was making a decision about where Austin was going to come from, I wanted him to come from the other side of the lake, which meant that he had to be an American. I wanted him to be part of a culture that was close enough to Canada to be able to move comfortably in the Canadian world as it existed then, but I also wanted him to be far enough away from Canada and from things Canadian to be able to look at it with detachment and as a tourist to a certain extent. For those reasons I knew he was going to be American. When I was beginning that novel I was thinking it might have to do with the Group of Seven and all of that, but it didn't work out that way. Things never do.

AC: It does relate in the sense of painting northern Canadian landscapes.

JU: That's the only thing that remained, really. And it became more interesting to me once I'd decided that he would be an American. At first I thought he might have gone to Canada and met up with Group members, but then I decided I wanted to see this place through his eyes.

I had an interesting dream. It had to do with the northern lake on which I was born, which had rocky outcroppings that went out in little peninsulas into the lake, and those little peninsulas had been carved. The back was all landscape, and the front was all battleship, and when I woke up I thought, what was all of that about? And I realized it's about exploitation. In a sense, while it's not necessarily a national allegory, Canada and the wilderness of Canada could be looked at as a metaphor for the feminine. And the exploitation of the feminine, while it's not necessarily an American thing, is somehow more believable as an American thing. And of course there is an awful lot of American exploitation of Canada, and particularly of natural resources.

But that wasn't really what I was trying to say. The primary theme, I think, was this kind of exploitation of the feminine. A Jungian that I know said of the feminine, you just rape her over and over, and he wasn't talking about women, but in the larger sense. If it exists, there should be some way to use it, which is the sensibility that seems to be predominant. So that's why – I mean obviously a Canadian could have done the same thing – I wanted him to come from a little further offshore, and I didn't want him involved in that work. And they weren't, until the last couple of years, with free trade. Rather like the War of 1812: they were there right from the beginning and won the whole thing themselves.

AC: I can see what you mean about there being many levels to the exploitation idea in the novel, because of the whole idea of natural resources, of which Sarah is one, and the beauty of the region particularly, being taken over in this very chilly style, which seems to have evolved through various art schools in the US.

JU: Art as exploitation, and that includes literature, was something that was on my mind quite a lot at that point, partly because of what has happened here in Canada in the literary world. Increasingly books are seen as products. Writers have been pretty heavily marketed in recent years, and I'm not sure that's the way it ought to be. I'm very torn about that because obviously you can't be unhappy about your own success, and success often involves all of that. But on the other hand I don't want to write a product. And I think you have to be constantly on guard not to have your work affected by this kind of marketing.

AC: I thought *The Underpainter* did develop a discussion around various forms of art and representation. You included an Ojibway legend and drew on the indigenous body of knowledge about a particular area.

JU: That's the area I was born near. So I knew the legends. The librarian in the tiny mining settlement where I was born also assisted me. And of course the sleeping giant does lie there.

AC: There's a parallel myth about the Cape Point area of Southern Africa, the Adamastor myth. I wondered why you describe an aboriginal as giving away the secret of the silver.

JU: Silver mining had gone on in that area, with the First Nations people, for thousands of years.

AC: They were the first miners in that area?

JU: Oh yes.

AC: Could you say something about underpainting as a metaphor or symbol in this novel? It does seem a very strange thing to do, to paint a realistic picture and then paint over it, or paint it out. I see you've spoken about this being very different from the Renaissance idea of underpainting. I interpreted the abstract technique that Austin develops, painting over a mimetic illusion, as a statement of the paradox of art, and perhaps as an expression of his cold personality. Is it also about the inevitable obliqueness of art?

JU: I think partly it was a reflection of his own character. It operated as a metaphor for memory as well, selective memory, which is also a part of his character.

AC: And especially with the distance in time at which he's telling his story.

JU: That's right. And also it was a kind of cathartic thing for him. He was really trying to get rid of all this material, there was no question about it. Sometimes when you write something out, you write it down – that's what the term means – it gets it out of you and onto the page. But he didn't want the painting hanging on the wall; there were a lot of things he was hoping to forget. I believe that has a lot to do with what the underpainting was about. As for the Renaissance term, underpainting just meant preparation of the canvas, usually done by studio technicians.

AC: It wasn't a whole picture?

JU: No. People just worked out the light and dark patterns, with the grand Maitre coming in to finish it all.

AC: I see. That's interesting, that you say it's related mainly to Austin's character, because of those opening scenes with his mother, where he's taken into these chilly tombs and graveyards, back to the undertaker idea. The child who is exposed to mortality; I can see the links here.

JU: The theory about those paintings, and about him, is that he was subjected to the fashion of the times as well, and began as a realist and moved through a Cubist phase for a while.

AC: He has this very detached attitude to his own career, summing up its phases.

JU: Yes, he has these ironic remarks now and then. By the time he's old, it's the seventies, and that kind of art would not have been that unusual in that period. In fact, I've had letters from actual painters who do "erasures" and who say things to me like, "Were you aware of my work?" Well, no. I had a lot of letters from the States.

AC: It was very convincing as a school of art.

JU: It's quite funny though, when you find that those paintings really do exist. We tried one in Tony's studio, to make sure you could technically do what I was explaining.

AC: You've mentioned L.M. Montgomery as a role model or inspiration for you; would you explain? Was it as a successful Canadian author, or the world of her fiction?

JU: It was a combination, I think. None of us believed, as children, that it was really possible for us, as Canadians on the one hand, and as women, on the other, to become a famous author. Now L.M. Montgomery had gone right out there and done that. That was a part of it. But also, she was writing about creative children, particularly the Emily books. They were pivotal. In fact, if you get the New Canadian Library editions of *Emily of New Moon*, the Afterword is by Alice Munro, the one to *Emily Climbs* is by me, and the one to *Emily's Quest* is by P.K. Page. And each of us responds to what it was about these books that intrigued us. They were novels about a young Canadian woman becoming an author.

AC: The childhood aspect was very important?

JU: Oh yes, absolutely.

AC: Was there any other Canadian writer who was especially important when you were setting out?

JU: Alice Munro, speaking as a reader. Her work has been terribly important to me as a reader. Probably as a writer as well, because she was able to be so successful in writing about her own place, her own geography. I think she's just brilliant.

AC: And she was able to say so much about women, the things that hadn't been said at all about women, so honestly.

JU: That's right. And in ways that were so human. You were looking from the inside out, and not the outside in. And I admire P.K. Page as well, and Alistair MacLeod. He's written perhaps only fifteen or sixteen stories, but even if he never writes anything else, those stories are extremely powerful. And Sheila Watson's *The Double Hook*. I remember sitting in a classroom right here, and coming across *The Double Hook* for the first time in 1969 or 1970. It gave me permission to go in all kinds of directions.

AC: Formally very innovative, you mean?

JU: Hugely. And especially coming out of what had been up until that time pretty dry stuff in Canada.

AC: Are you happy to be associated with a group of writers who practise Southern Ontario Gothic literature (Robertson Davies, Atwood, Findley, Munro)? I can see Munro sometimes writing in that mode, with her use of murders and the grotesque. You do create ghosts, but they're quite nice, refined ghosts. Do you feel yourself to be working in any Canadian literary tradition?

JU: I do have a tendency to be more interested in the dark than in the light. I can't remember where that term came from. I think it was Atwood.

AC: Well, Atwood's *Alias Grace* certainly fits the description, those bodies in the cellar.

JU: I think she actually coined the phrase.

AC: Maybe. It's a very useful phrase. I like it.

JU: I do too.

AC: But I wondered how you felt about being placed in any kind of tradition of Canadian writing, or do you see yourself as working in isolation?

JU: I think probably more the latter than the former, which doesn't mean I don't feel I'm part of a community of Canadian writers, because I am. It's partly just circumstantially, where I've lived, and where I've chosen to live. I tend to choose to live in villages. I partly grew up in the north, and partly in Toronto. Even when I lived in Toronto there was the alternative of the village, where my extended family lived. I guess I would prefer to think of myself as working in isolation, but I suspect that's true of most authors.

AC: I can't readily link your work with any line of writers, whereas some writers are deliberately writing back to a tradition.

JU: It's a solitary activity for me; I'm protective of it. I like the idea that it's all mine.

AC: And there's the localized research that you do, which is quite distinctive.

JU: Yes, and that's a big part of the creative process for me, and terribly exciting. So I imagine now that it's difficult to place my work in any larger context, but it may not be later, when we pull back a little more and see what's been going on in Canada.

AC: Well, I can see certain parallels with Janice Kulyk Keefer's work, the use of a female researcher figure, and working through certain British texts of authors, but I couldn't see any obvious Canadian links.

JU: I certainly think of myself that way, and I like the idea of swimming in unknown waters.

AC: Yes, and the idea of an alternative world. Each of your books seems to invent a whole alternative world.

JU: Which reminds me, I should tell you the French linguistics story. And this applies to *The Whirlpool*. When it was first published the book met with no response, despite the fact that it was published by McLelland and Stewart. This was in 1985. It came out in October, and nothing happened. Nothing good, nothing bad. Then finally after about four months there was a tiny little review in a publication called *Quill and Quire*. One always remembers one's bad reviews. The reviewer said it was an ill-digested mish-mash of grim Canadian themes and French linguistic theory. At that point, up to my neck in diapers, I had no idea what this phrase meant. I thought, I remember taking linguistics at university, and I figured, what has this to do with linguistics? As for French linguistic theory, I'd never heard of it. I lived through that review, and then the book finally did get some attention. Then it got more and more attention, and eventually it was published in France. And in France it was published in the Lettres Nouvelles series. And miraculously it won the Prix du Meilleur Livre Etranger. But what was funny about that was that the jury was comprised of thirteen of France's best-known linguistic theorists.

AC: Maybe that review was the making of you, then?

JU: I don't think it was the making of me so much, but the person must have had a point somewhere along the line, because the French linguists just adored it.

AC: I'll have to read it again. But it's good that it won the prize. Good to have the recognition.

JU: It was wonderful, fabulous.

AC: But you never know how your work is going to be received. It is strange that they set up such a theoretical framework when it was the last thing you were proceeding from.

How do you hope to make all of your analogies with and descriptions of visual art work in your fiction? You mention some influence from your husband's worldview as a painter. How did this work for you?

JU: Travelling with him was very important, just because you can't help but start to look at the world through the eyes of a person who is more visual than verbal. That was fabulous training for me. But I also think that even before I knew Tony I was always drawn to images. And so the visual was a part of my sensibility from the beginning, not that I consider myself a visual artist in any way, because I certainly don't. I use that eye when I'm writing, the same eye you might use for photography.

AC: Do you keep journals?

JU: Oh yes, I do. I keep big scrapbook journals; I paste things in. There's a diary side to them, in that I record things if I find them particularly funny, or arresting. But it's also just scraps of things that I come across that I want to write about or just play with. I make collage-type images. I've done that ever since I was a little kid, and still really enjoy it. It's great fun. I keep them in big black scrapbooks.

AC: So they're source books for you then?

JU: Not really.

AC: They're separate from your writing? You don't use them directly?

JU: Sometimes. And sometimes things appear in the scrapbooks that also appear in my writing, but I don't necessarily use them as something on which to draw.

AC: You've spoken of the consumerist trend in the literary world. You've worked in the public realm as a lecturer, creative writing teacher, and a writer-in-residence. How have these activities affected your writing life?

JU: First of all, part of what was wonderful about them was that they were finite experiences. It wasn't as if I got a job at the university as a professor or lecturer and that was going to be my life. These were things I did for three or four months. And I always enjoyed them. I found, much to my surprise, that I would get more of my creative work done when I was a writer-in-residence than I did when my life was completely unstructured. I have a great fear and distrust of structured time, so I will never discipline myself within a structure. But when I'm in a situation where my commitments demand that I be within a structure, I actually function rather well. It's one of those paradoxes.

AC: There's another side of the constraint and control idea.

JU: But I always think that when someone comes to me with something that they've written, one has to be aware that the quality of the piece is almost irrelevant. Someone is bringing you their heart in their hands, and I've always enjoyed dealing with that aspect of things. Essentially you have an intimate connection with a stranger in that way that you can't really get in any other way, and I think that's an extension of reading for me. I've enjoyed that very much. I still believe, though, that it's impossible to teach creative writing. And I don't think that I, who never studied creative writing, suffered in any way.

AC: You weren't actually teaching creative writing; you were responding in a workshop situation?

JU: That's right. And personally, on a one to one basis. I had an office and people would make appointments. And I also have a very difficult time believing that people who have been through schools of creative writing were more likely to become writers than anyone else. Having said that, there's also that wonderful thing that happens, which is what I've found exciting about being in a position to teach creative writing, and that was the ability to encourage something you see in an infant state, and also to expose the student to other things, even just to direct their reading, or give them competence in areas they might not have had before. Yes, I liked it.

AC: Would you say a little about your current writing project? Has there been any change of focus or direction for you as a novelist recently?

JU: I thought the biggest shift I'd ever taken in my life was into, first of all, the first-person, and secondly, the male voice for *The Underpainter*. But what I'm doing now may be an even bigger shift than that, in that my protagonist is a very strong, domineering woman. And she's fascinating. Again, it's a historical framework, and I can't say that much about it because I'm halfway through and I feel I might jinx it if I talk about it, and also it could change radically before it ever gets near the press, if it ever does. But there's a suggestion of a woman who is going to take control of things, and I don't think I've ever written about that before.

It's set again in Ontario, taking place sometime between the wars, mostly, though there's a certain section dealing with the developments of the village in which the woman lives, and that takes place in the nineteenth century. It involves another immigrant group, and this time it's German immigrants. That's about all I can tell you at this stage, except that it has to do with structure, with building things, one of which is a big cathedral that was built in the wilderness north of Stratford. The other thing I'm very interested in is the Vichy memorial. We shall see how it shakes down.

AC: As you say, that was a big change, quite a radical experiment for you, to write a first-person male narrative. You use the graphic phrase, "a necklace of narrative", in *The Underpainter*.

JU: It was interesting for me to do it because I was surprised at how easily that voice came to me. And how authentic it felt. I didn't have any trouble getting inside his mind at all.

AC: Thank you very much. Would you mind reading a poem from *The Little Flowers of madame de Montespan*?

"Venetian Gondoliers at Versailles"

I. Their republic opened out toward the sea. Long fingers extended to the lagoon. They returned by different routes in a city like a maze.

II. Here they sail over a false lake, a captive canal. Still waters go nowhere. They encounter edges. Women won't call to them from balconies. No one speaks of flowers... or the moon.

III. And winter comes too soon. Skins bleach. Bones swell up with dampness and the cold. Boats are frozen in a corner of the garden.

IV. They wish for raw confusion. Buildings that pressure back the sun; bridges that teem with circumstances. Not the knives of the doctors, bleeding winter diseases, the cold eyes of women bored by the court.

V. Sometimes at night they dream that their bloodstreams have become canals, moving outwards, to the sea. Their lost city, carried here inside the prison of their bodies.

VI. They've forgotten the songs they used to sing.

Subverting Canadian Suburbia: Barbara Gowdy

Barbara Gowdy is a Toronto novelist and short story writer. Born in Don Mills, Ontario, she has established the bizarre as an avenue into understanding "normal" Canadian family life. Her Canadian fictions imply that it is not immigrant and minority life that is strange and problematic in Canada, but mainstream European settler suburban life.

After a first novel, *Through the Green Valley* (1989), a historical romance, she established her reputation in the story collections *Falling Angels* (1989) and *We So Seldom Look on Love* (1992). Gowdy's 1996 novel, *Mister Sandman*, was nominated for the Governor-General's Award for Fiction, the Giller Prize, and the Trillium Award. Later fictions include *The White Bone* (1999), *The Romantic* (2003), *Helpless* (2007) and *Little Sister* (2017).

In her innovative novel, *The White Bone* (1998), Gowdy creates and inhabits an entire mythic matriarchal world of African elephants. The world of elephants functions lyrically as an archetype of social relations, kinship and shared memory. The elephants' quest for a safe place becomes an image of our human and social quest for shared meaning and value within the global village at the turn of the millennium.

Interview with Barbara Gowdy

AC: Your story collection set in the sixties, *Falling Angels*, represents adolescence, families and first experiences of sexuality in disturbing terms of extreme authoritarianism and lovelessness. Are these extremes of unpleasantness ways of exploring the distortions of fixed social and familial codes, or simply ways of registering extremes in human behaviour?

BG: I would contend with the lovelessness. The sisters love each other desperately. There's only one authoritarian figure, the father. They love their mother desperately, and she loves them. She's incapable, but there's probably more love between them than there is in most families. There's an authoritarian father, but even he loves them, looks after them, doesn't take off.

That was partly an investigation of that particular time, which was very patriarchal. It was a bankrupt generation of men who came back from World War II and were trying to create order and meaning in their lives after an experience in which there was no order and meaning, namely war.

Growing up as a girl in the fifties, I found is a difficult time to be a female, and a difficult time to be a certain kind of female, being thin and intellectually minded. And I had no real heroines or figures to admire who were anything like me. You didn't hear about strong women, certainly not the way you hear about them today: women with power, good jobs, minds. I can remember being told by a high school teacher that only girls who can't get married go to university.

AC: Oh yes, those messages were very strong then.

BG: So if there was any ranting in that book, it was a rant against that time. I decided it couldn't be unremittingly dark; that's not how I see the world anyway. So there's a lot of dark humour in the book, and the humour was a way of leavening the events, but also a way of throwing things into relief. Humour – the best humour – turns everything upside down and forces you to see things differently, so humour was a way of shedding light on certain of those events. The events are extreme, I guess, but I was just focussing on the extreme. There's nothing in that book that couldn't happen, hasn't happened, isn't probably happening right now, when we think about it. Except there's probably no one down in a bomb shelter right now, but who knows, they do exist.

AC: In that same collection you also draw on the genre of interlinked short stories and the portrayal of one family at different times. Were you responding to earlier examples of this genre in Canada or anywhere else?

BG: No, I felt very uninfluenced. Everyone thinks I've read stuff I haven't read or authors I haven't even heard of. But the family just quite separately intrigues me, and I return to it again and again in all my fiction. I think it's because the family has always struck me as a complete social entity, a foreign country in fact, ruled by the parents, either benevolently or not. The family is either democracy or dictatorship, monarchy. And the kids, at least in the house I grew up in, have their separate bedrooms, and those are like little nation states. When you go into another house, everything is completely different. It's like a foreign country; the smells are completely different, the customs, the food, the power structures. I think that women writers know – or women know – that if you get the family right you get the world right. And that's where female power is.

AC: Or female powerlessness.

BG: True, but it's still not quite out there in the world. I found myself thinking, with the current war in Yugoslavia, where's feminism in all this? The pictures of women you see are just of desperate women with their ravaged eyes. The men are doing the ethnic cleansing, the men are the dictators, the soldiers, the ambassadors. There's only Madeleine Albright, and sometimes I wonder if she is a woman. So I did wonder about feminism and women in big events; we seem to recede. But in really important events, the so-called small events, which are the genesis, the household, where we come from, there we are.

And it especially interested me growing up where I did, which is Canada, a cold country, so you're inside a lot, in a suburb not yet a community, no malls then. You go from one pod, which is highly populated, because most people have three of four kids, to another pod. You moved between these pods where families operated, and it was a constellation of nations, it seemed to me.

AC: I like that focus on the family, because it says so much. That's where everything happens, especially for people under twenty-one. That's their whole terrain.

BG: Over twenty-one, too. I don't think you ever escape your family.

AC: Yes, families do go on forever.

So there weren't particular models for you? That was just your way of proceeding?

BG: Yes.

AC: In *We So Seldom Look on Love*, you seem to turn the idea of freaks into a literary vehicle: doubled-up people in "Sylvie" and "The Two-Headed Man", exhibitionists and necrophiliacs. Would you talk about this literary preoccupation with physical deformity in the stories? What is it meant to convey about human experience, or about contemporary society?

BG: There are freaks in some of those stories, not all of them, maybe not even half of them. I was looking at them last night, and I was thinking that they're all more shocking in execution than in description, because whatever's going to happen in that story I tell you right up front and then I just try to familiarize you with it. Every one of those stories is based on something I heard or read, and usually how it works out – what the necrophile does, or how the babies come out of two wombs – that's based on real life. There was a real freak who exhibited and married a doctor.

I often only think later what I was up to. I try to work as unconsciously as possible. I try to inform myself about the world and then work unconsciously. Really ultra-conscious writing doesn't appeal to me that much. Its agenda is a little suspect, I think.

It occurs to me later that what I was doing in those stories was turning the short story on its head, especially the Canadian short story, the Alice Munro mode, where something very normal is investigated and the extraordinary is extracted. I was taking the extraordinary and saying, "Look upon it long enough – we so seldom look on love – and it will normalize for you." That's because everybody in their own culture thinks they're perfectly normal; they come to another culture, where everything's changed, and they just don't get it. "We are normal, you are abnormal."

That contest, which is at the root of all hatred, all war, all insecurity, doesn't have to be there. These are huge leaps in empathy for me, constantly, standing in shoes that I've never been in, that I don't want to be in, that I know nothing about, researching them, thinking about them, saying that I'm going to put myself in their situation, hypothetically. I'm going to take my heart and put it in this person's body, though it might be a body that repulses me. Although one thing I was also conscious of doing was never writing about someone I felt was reprehensible, people without conscience or kindness. Those people, the Paul Bernardos of this world, don't interest me. I think they're brain damaged to the point of being uninteresting, that they literally have a screw loose. So that's not interesting in fiction.

But the characters in this book, they're people we may flinch from, but that's not fair, because they're not bad people; they're different people. And that was my investigation at that time. It was a kind of cry on behalf of difference, and a real rage against the pernicious idea of normalcy. I say pernicious, of course, because there's no such thing. It changes from time to time and culture to culture.

There's also an increasing pressure or trend now, for people to become normal. It's always been a desire, but now it's possible to alter your looks, including men. Certain actors, like Michael Jackson, tried to look like blond actresses in LA, or behave like that. I worship at the altar of diversity, and that really upsets me. So that was also behind that book, that rage.

AC: Yes, against the normative pressure, which has been so damaging for women, particularly, but of course here in Canada, too.

BG: For everyone who comes here.

AC: Exactly.

BG: I heard a young girl of about fourteen. I think she was Sri Lankan, with a very strong accent. I thought, she's about twelve, she'll lose that accent so quickly, and she'll be able to because of her age. But it was so charming for me, painful for her, to hear it.

AC: Your fiction is anti-incorporation, anti any automatic assimilation into North America?

BG: What's there to look at if there's a plain blank screen? What's there to write about when everything's the same?

AC: But it's also about victimhood in a sense, because of the kinds of people you're writing about. They do express a kind of vulnerability which is greater than the groups who are always claiming victimhood.

BG: What I always find rather touching is that those who are true victims often can't talk about it, or don't talk about it much. They often get ignored, and a lot of them are children. People who work at children's hospitals talk about how brave the children are. It doesn't occur to them to start claiming compensation. They just have an animal urge to live, to get by, and to be optimistic. And people who've really suffered deeply don't get up in front of the TV cameras and whine about it. They can't.

AC: That's right.

BG: And they're the ones who appeal to my sympathies, and I try to give voice to those people. I consider myself a leap of imagination writer. I don't use the cold hard facts of my own life like a lot of writers do, with great effect. But it just doesn't seem to work for me, and my interest lies elsewhere. You have to write about what interests you.

AC: Oh yes, certainly.

BG: And my interest is really in people who are completely different from me. That's why I've written in the voices of gay men, great big fat women, children, every different sort of human being you can imagine. And I've gone further, into the animal world, which is really a natural evolution.

AC: At first I thought *The White Bone* seemed a radically different book from your earlier ones, but when I worked my way back and read the earlier collections I could see how that exploration of difference might naturally lead a writer to that kind of novel, or romance, about animals. But there's also the physicality of your people as a link. I'm thinking of your stories now. It's a very physical thing if you have two pairs of legs or two heads. It adds a concreteness to experience.

BG: It's also a frankness. We say, "I have to go to the loo." How about, "I have to go and move my bowels in the bathroom?" What is wrong with that?

AC: Language is full of euphemisms.

BG: We gentle everything, we seldom say what we mean. And that's very confusing for children. You get the wrong message all the time because we're incapable of being frank, and we decide that certain things can be said and others can't. It's quite arbitrary.

AC: It's a strike against euphemism as well, and the softsoaping of language.

BG: And even the lyrical metaphor that doesn't tell you anything. I use metaphors, but I try to make them sharp and clear and use them to fine-tune the focus, rather than to muddy the focus. I really try hard. It's tempting to use metaphor for effect. Because a lot of people think, "Oh, this must be a literary novel, it's replete with metaphors. I could do that. Metaphor time!" But I rail against that in fiction in my own work. I want the truth. I've written five books now, and I'm trying to start something new. I haven't yet had the time to do it. But I think my challenge now will be, really consciously, to write a clear and truthful sentence. That is so hard.

AC: Well, I think you succeed. I liked the ending of *Falling Angels*, when the dead mother turns into a seagull and says to her daughter, "You are on your own now. The world is all yours. Your father is the fish I ate." I think the stories are very strong, and *The White Bone* is beautiful, very concrete.

BG: It is very concrete, but then it is to them, the elephants. I tried to write from their point of view. They would see things not as we see them, and they would flinch at things we don't flinch at. They would engage the world with far less fear and repulsion than we would, because they actually eat the world. Whether we eat take-outs from a supermarket or dine at a restaurant, it's not gnawing at the earth, or at a tree. Their relationship to reality is so basic, and at the same time so complex.

AC: In *The White Bone* one gets the physical recycling in which animals are part of the world, but also their eons of memory make that world very rich spiritually.

A number of your stories, and the novel *Mister Sandman*, explore sexuality, the wayward and comical nature of sexual desire, truthfulness versus the desire for absolute love. That novel is wonderfully funny, I laughed a lot, but there's a painful edge to a lot of those situations. How do you view the role of eroticism and sexuality in fiction? I thought "Sylvie", for instance, was about the nature of female orgasm, and the desire women perhaps feel to have the singleness of male sexual pleasure, rather than the penis Freud told us we secretly desired. The image of two sets of legs conveys something about the doubleness of female sexual identity. Then at the end of the story one set of legs is going to be removed! I think women are haunted by the idea that sexual response should be single, but of course for women it isn't.

BG: There really was a four-legged woman who exhibited in Barnum's circus, but I removed that time frame. There are pictures of her. What's interesting about her is that, first of all, she didn't have to exhibit. She could have hidden her deformity under the full skirts they wore at the time.

AC: Which is how the story begins.

BG: So why did she? And she was married to a doctor, so it wasn't required. She seemed to like to have her picture taken with her dress lifted, showing her little stocking on her little legs, surrounded by her children. The story is she had three out of one vagina, two out of the other. I remember the first thing I thought when I looked at that picture. I looked at the legs and thought, how interesting, and then my eyes were riveted by the doctor, the husband. Who the hell's he? And what's he up to? The story has an obvious feminist message. Men want the tiger in the bedroom, apparently, and the lady in the living room. Well, too bad. Why should I be schizophrenic to serve your agenda?

AC: Well, you'd think a woman with four legs and two vaginas would fulfil more than one need for the husband.

BG: I didn't mention it, but two periods, too, which probably didn't coincide. In those days they didn't have all the benefits of mini and maxi-pads. It must have been horrible. Does Barbie have a period? Barbie has a calendar. I always think they should mark off the days of her periods. But it's the same thing. The husband was attracted to her; he was excited by the four legs, but he had to have the extra set removed, because they weren't normal, they didn't suit the idea of a wife. And it's left as an open question at the end of the story, whether this is going to be a happy marriage. But it was told from her point of view because she's the poignant one in the story. Also, I create her, as I often do when I deal with mothers and sisters, as having a sister, which is her legs, so really she's an unformed Siamese twin, but only the legs grew. And the mother in that story is far more doting upon the little legs, the sister who never was, the potential sister.

AC: Yes, real sisters and daughters are more problematic.

BG: I often have in my stories, I realized, children who die and could have been gods, children who aren't quite formed and could have been "the one". And here's a child having to overcome that hurt of not being adored, the Christ-figure child that every pregnant woman hopes she will have. Sylvie has to deal not only with the sexuality in her life, but the duality in her life, who she is, should have been, could have been, who she partly is.

AC: There's a structural metaphor of doubleness in those stories which seems to be about the duality of female experience. But in that story it's particularly clear.

BG: "The Two-Headed Man" is not about women at all. That was based on a story I heard on the radio. There are instances of people born with two heads, but usually it's a real vestigial head that can't do anything but loll. This story was about a head that did talk and did think, and then the body in control, the main head, cut it off because it was an abusive head, and was charged not with suicide but with murder. I don't believe this really happened, but it became an urban myth story that people claimed they heard on TV or in China. What was interesting to me was not so much even the duality of sexuality as the duality of personality. Who am I, privately, publically?

AC: Duality of identity too, yes. You have another story with identical twin brothers, and a girl who has sex with both. The people we have sex with are always more than one person, or the people we see are always more than one person.

BG: We have these shimmering selves around us, but there's only one that seems to do all the talking. But there are others, and we have to contend with all of those others.

AC: They should tell that to hiring committees; it might help me get a real job. Hey, I'm really six people.

BG: And I'd really love the other five, if they would only shut up.

AC: I would just need six people's salary.

Would you say more about the Canary family in *Mister Sandman*? Homosexuality is another expression of difference. Parents who become homosexual in later life are not uncommon now, or perhaps they just live their lives more openly, when their lives and partnerships change. In *Mister Sandman* you really do explore the amorphousness of sexual identity.

BG: Sex concerns me as a writer not in terms of how people do it, we all know what happens, but sexual identity, because we're all so overwrought about it. And I think I have a nature that likes to pick scabs, look in dark corners, clean out cupboards. You don't find any dirt in my cupboards because I find it myself. It's the same with sex. What is it with humans and sexuality? Because you don't find it in the animal world, this obsession. Why are we so strange, and overwrought, and upset about it?

AC: Partly because of the family structure you outlined, the way it's been set up from way back when, as normative.

BG: Then why even that? Where did it start? Why has it got to this? And so I don't declare anything in my fiction. I don't figure anything out. I just decide to investigate it. And most of my fiction comes from the question: what if? What if I were a four-legged woman, or a gay man? And then I try and imagine that. In this story, *Mister Sandman* – I think every family has its secrets; if they are foreign countries, they are the ones with secret services all over the place – I ask: what if a family's secrets, and I made them all rather shocking, all came out all at once to every member of the family?

You see these people on TV who find out their husbands did this or their son did that, and they're often shocked, but they often stick by the person, too, their mass-murdering son and so on. I decided that in this family, first of all, the secrets would not be harmful to one another, as sexual secrets between consenting adults very rarely are. And that there would be enough love in the family to survive the revelations of its secrets. But they would be stunning secrets, and I wasn't sure what they would be, so I worked that out.

But I knew that there would be a force, like Joan, because Joan is the hearth of the family, they sit around and tell her their secrets. But she would also be this cleansing force. With her initials, it did occur to me, she's a kind of Jesus Christ, the confessor. She takes everything in and shines it back out as a kind of light. It's so funny, I thought that symbolism was really clear, but no one picked that up. Except in ways I didn't intend. All my intended symbolism – though I hate that phrase – wasn't picked up.

I was interviewed by a gay woman, and she said, "So sexual problems come out of the closet? Joan had lived in a closet, this little girl liked to spend most of her time in the closet. She absorbed the secrets and sent them back out, so she took everyone out of the closet." And the closet metaphor had never occurred to me. That's not why she was in the closet.

AC: No, I didn't see it that way either. I saw her as fulfilling many different roles in the family. She is a lightening rod for everything that happens.

BG: As the family dog often is. That's why she's mute. People who don't talk a lot are often invested by their listeners with a great deal of intelligence. And people invest their dogs with skills, too. "That dog reads my mind. That dog is psychic." And in a way Joan's muteness allows them to invest her with a kind of holiness and insightfulness.

AC: Also, if one believes in these Freudian structures, she's interesting in that she has two mothers, one putative and one actual, who are both in the same family, so she's a child of incest in a sense. A very interesting symbolic figure in terms of biology and culture.

BG: I didn't want that to be too heavy-handed.

AC: No, it isn't.

BG: You know what else is funny about her. Everything she does leads people to call her an autistic child. She exhibits autistic behaviour. I didn't know anything about autistic children. Somehow, I invented an autistic child, with hypersensitivity. I didn't know that, but then I read about it later, when everyone said, "Joan's autistic."

AC: I don't know about it either. But one often finds such a figure in women's fiction, an autistic or crazy girl, because I think women writers explore these different layers of consciousness, and the autistic girl may be the layer damaged or silenced by a male-dominated culture. In that family, it's amazing how much thought and emotion is invested in Joan because she doesn't speak, because she's always there, a figure to confess to.

I was interested in the idea of extra-sensory perception, or telepathy, because you take that further later with the elephants in *The White Bone*.

BG: It's just communication, how we communicate. I don't have any evidence for ESP, telepathy, or visionary capabilities. And yet, all through time and culture we've had a sense of this. We're always sensing it, looking for it, but we don't quite grasp it. It occurred to me that in *The White Bone* I gave the elephants telepathy and visionary powers partly because it opens up a realm where they can communicate with other species, and to have a sense of what's happening far away, the way we can use television and radio. But also, I hypothesized that if we feel there's telepathy in the universe or the ether, maybe we're only brute enough to sense its presence, but not to actually have it. And it might be there in animals as a matter of course, and it might not be. But we don't know.

And what I was doing in this book, by gifting my elephants with very high intentions, high philosophy and sensitivity, was saying, look, we don't know who you are. This book is presumptuous and flawed, but this is a way of communicating that you are way more than we know, and I will give you what I can, as far as the powers that I can command, but I imagine that the powers you do have are completely other. This is the best that I can offer.

AC: I think telepathy relates to memory, may be just another name for memory, and the way we communicate with those who are not physically around us, whom we remember even if they're people we saw yesterday. There's a reel of images that runs through our minds.

BG: Memory is certainly a huge part of *The White Bone*, what I was thinking about when I was writing it.

AC: Do you think of yourself as responding to or subverting clean cut nuclear family advertising and stereotyping, or moral rearmament, or Christian ideas of moral norms for behaviours?

BG: No one forces you to join a church, especially in this country, unless you're a little kid. We force the church to be what we need it to be, and it's so far removed from spirituality. That's why it scares me. The real work of answering the question, who am I and what is the universe, and what is the appropriate way to live, given that life involves so much pain, and loss – those questions don't seem to be asked by many religions, so they frighten me. Organized religions just have lots of rules to keep the religion intact. I'm partly anti-religion because it's often anti-art, and I consider myself an artist. I've also been told I'm a witch. Someone worked out my astrological chart and said, "You were burned as a witch in your previous life."

What scares me about religion is, first of all, it's rigid and prohibitive, and, secondly, it's so far removed from the basic, innocent questions we ask of the world and need answers to, and we don't get those answers there. I get them more from literature and philosophy than religion. I went to the Presbyterian Church when I was growing up, and the only thing of value that I got was the hymns. You notice that my elephants sing hymns that are vaguely Presbyterian.

AC: Those were marvellous. I loved those elephant songs.

Does the distinction between Canadian and American literature have any significance for you? I can see affiliations with American writers like Vonnegut, for instance, in your use of absurdity, grotesquerie, black humour as social critique, but it doesn't seem to be much of a tradition in Canada.

BG: No, I don't think it is. It's happening, though. There's so much being written right now.

AC: I'm thinking of the earlier period. There doesn't seem to be much tradition of black humour.

BG: There wasn't much literature until about thirty years ago.

AC: Perhaps, but the humour of someone like Stephen Leacock is made up of village observations, the humour of the parochial. Do you see yourself as affiliated with American literature? Does the national category of Canadian literature have any meaning or value for you?

BG: No, it doesn't. I've read a lot, and probably I've been greatly influenced by writers, but I'm not conscious of it. Probably the only conscious connection I have is a sense of permission: if there is black humour, I can also write it. I think that probably why we haven't had such strategies is because new countries are too insecure to poke fun at themselves. You need a kind of security for that to happen. You need a physical, economic, and social security, all of which I had. With this country at war, which it had been for about ten years, black humour had no place. And even in The *White Bone* it's gone. There's some humour, but I wouldn't say it's black humour. When you're writing about a species that's being slaughtered and on the verge of extinction, it's not appropriate.

AC: I was thinking of your earlier stories.

BG: I know, but I want to make the comparison. The reason it's not in *The White Bone* is because elephants are at war. They're being slaughtered; life is insecure. There's no room for black humour, or glibness, or even short snappy sentences in that kind of world. If my experience of the world were that of the elephants, I couldn't have written the way I did. The style serves the subject, and my subjects have invited a black humour style, whereas that subject didn't.

But as I say, there was a permission to write in that way because of a security. I live in an individualist society. I'm not going to get arrested for what I write. No one's going to stop me writing. In fact they give me grants. I have a certain economic stability, and if I didn't I could get unemployment insurance. Nobody starves here.

AC: It's partly a generation difference, then?

BG: It's partly the age of the country. Literature evolves through decades. New literature is often rather derivative. What I find interesting is that Alice Munro, Margaret Atwood, and Carol Shields started out as strong writers – how did they get so good so early? Where do they come from? That's more interesting than where I come from. They are the sediment, in a way. I remember reading Carol Shields decades ago and thinking, why isn't she more famous?

Ann Clayton

She's so good. Where did she come from? Why was *Lives of Girls and Women* such a great book? How did Margaret Atwood write what she did? She has a dark sensibility; she was one of the first. If I think about it, she was probably the one who gave me most permission to go a little down that road.

AC: Yes, she has a similar world, especially in her treatment of the family and adolescence.

BG: She must have felt like an outsider, growing up in the north, in the woods, then coming into the city.

AC: Yes, I think she has said so. But did you feel yourself to be an outsider?

BG: As a female in the fifties, I did.

AC: Right. Being an intellectual in the Barbie doll era.

BG: No breasts, when Marilyn Monroe was the icon.

AC: And non-conformist.

You've spoken about how *The White Bone* developed out of your earlier work. What made you decide to write such a complete rendering of an elephant world, to explore that terrain in a form of science fiction, or mythic fantasy? That book crosses a lot of genre boundaries.
BG: First of all, writing about animals is just an extension of writing about what's not known to me, what's at the edge of human experience. Animals are not normal humans. But also, my amateur interest is in animals, zoology. I wished for some time of my life that I'd been a zoologist, or at least a vet, forgetting how much work you have to do.

AC: You could come to Guelph to study vet science. We have no elephants on campus. It would be rather nice to have a few wandering around.

BG: I'm an autodidact and have a very hard time with structured learning, so I would never get a degree. I have occasionally taught; it's not that I don't believe in it. You don't have to write about what you know; I don't do it. You use what you know as the furniture, to get the emotions and the room right, but as far as your subject matter goes, write about what really interests and obsesses you, if something does, because you'll return to that.

For me it was family, and the elephants are also families, matriarchies. A reviewer in England, by the way, in *The Spectator*, wouldn't read past the first nineteen pages. He said, "This has to be a feminist diatribe, because she has matriarchies and a female god." The reason I have matriarchies is that there are matriarchies in the real world, and I made a female god because it seemed to me if I'm going to give them a cosmology – in their world the females do rule, they're the bosses – that they wouldn't have a male god. But these are families, and I write about families.

AC: And about survival.

BG: Yes, survival, and the reason for elephants is just that at the time I was considering writing a book from the point of view of an animal. Not for the sake of emulating human behaviour through the vehicle of an animal, but doing what I do, which is getting inside their skins and imagining their world, which is an exciting prospect for me. I picked elephants because at that time I'd seen a documentary on elephants, and I became fascinated by them, started reading about them.

They're so smart; they're so intelligent, but I thought I could also interest the reader in their lives, because they do have a language, which the scientists call vocalization. They do have big, complex brains, complex societies, similar lifespans to humans. They get arthritis and cardiovascular diseases. Their brains grow. In short, they have a lot in common with humans. Their brains grow 67% from infancy to adulthood; ours grow 70%. So there's a lot of soft wiring; they have to learn how to be elephants, which is good fictional information, because learning is part of changing. An ant or a lizard is not going to have the same behaviour as an animal that learns and adapts its behaviour depending on circumstances. That makes for very interesting fiction.

That's why elephants started to come into my story, and part of my fascination, apart from their intelligence, is the fact that they are imperilled. And their relationships with us are so interesting. They know that we're the enemy, we're killing them, and yet when they come across humans the feel they can trust, they do trust them. If they were a species built on our annihilation, as we're bent on theirs, they wouldn't take certain individuals into consideration. In a war we don't say, "Now that Serb soldier is gentle and a poet, so I won't shoot him." But animals aren't like us.

AC: I thought, because of the famous *Heart of Darkness*, and Europeans going to central Africa for ivory, that they serve as quite a potent symbol of any colonized group, or a species that's robbed because of colonialism. And also it seemed to give you a lot of range for inventiveness, with the names, the genealogies, the language, the communication system.

BG: Well, there was no elephant going to write a critique in the *New York Review of Books* to tell me how wrong I was. But I do think that when you imagine another life, you should do your research, so I did as much as I could and then came out with something completely presumptuous. In England, I've had the hardest time with reviewers. Someone said, "How do you know, when you have them singing, where did that come from?" This is not a scientific treatise. This is imagined reality, for one thing, but even that is based on something real.

Joyce Pool, who's worked with Cynthia Moss – they have these natural history names – in Africa for about thirty years, has studied animal communication and vocalization. She says she's seen elephants walking about at night, swaying their trunks, and she says she could swear they were singing. So I said, well, I'm a fiction writer, so they're singing. That's what I get to do. And it's funny, but with this book I've had to defend my credentials, defend my imagination, strangely.

AC: Perhaps ecologists, naturalists, feel you're treading on their territory.

BG: It's not naturalists. It's book reviewers. It's not anyone who knows anything about elephants. In fact, the reviews in Canada and the States were great. In England they were mixed, and when they were negative the issue has been: what right do I have to do this? I haven't lived for very long among elephants. I'm not a zoologist. Why are the elephants talking? It should be a social parody or something else.

AC: But I think the elephants are also important because their world is one of ritual. They seem to have many rituals, and they grieve like humans. They have this world of ritualized emotions which you were partly drawing on, partly creating.

What about memory, and the feminism in the novel? Was your creation of a matriarchal world a conscious counter-statement to a culture that is still largely created by men?

BG: No. They're matriarchies because they're matriarchies. That's it. As far as memory goes, though, it became a huge concern for me in the book, because apparently it's true that they never forget. People who work with them think there are both physiological and behavioural elements to support that conjecture. I found myself wondering what it would be like never to forget, and more importantly, never to be able to forget, which is a more crucial concern, because shame and pain or two things we like to wipe off our slates, and can do fairly effectively. What if you couldn't? And I think that's a real moral question.

AC: Therapy is partly about changing memory.

BG: Well, say your memory is perfect, you haven't altered anything, as we do, with our imperfect memories. And of course what I think is that elephants are more moral than we are. They're more gentle, and forgiving, and less vengeful because they have long, long memories.

I was promoting this book in the States, when the children went into a school at Littleton and shot thirteen or fourteen fellow students, and people at the time were questioning why they would do this. Was it the violent videos? Was it bad parenting? I wanted to throw it into the pot: I think it's a lack of memory. I think it's the fact that especially young people today don't have much of a cultural memory, or geographic, historical, social memory.

AC: They haven't lived through a war, either.

BG: They don't even know who the president was before Clinton. Very few of them could tell you that. They don't seem to be learning this. I don't know why it's not taught. And when you have no memory, when you live in an eternal present, when everything before or to come is to feed into that eternal present, you are in a morally bankrupt position, because you have no sense of consequence, or perspective. I think that's what memory gives us, and I think the more perfect our memories, and the longer they are, the better we'd be.

AC: Because we remember what causes damage?

BG: We understand consequence and we have perspective. We remember our own beginnings.

AC: Do you think writing extends the bounds of human community?

BG: Sure it does, not because there's a specific social or political agenda. Fiction comes from too deep a place to pollute it with that. But if you're just trying to investigate the world, using the word, the experience of story, to crack open the world that you know, then what happens for the writer, anyway, is that you do extend your own experience by imagining others. I've become more empathetic by trying to imagine different people's experiences. If the book works, it should crack open the heart of the reader a little bit. That's what fiction can do. There's a lot of very intellectual fiction that's afraid to have too much emotion in it. Many Canadian male writers are rather good at that, because other men like it. But if you do have emotion, or sentiment, it's called over-emotional, unintelligent, female. And yet one of the things fiction can do is crack open your heart. It also cracks open your brain a little, but non-fiction can also do that. There's something fiction can do to move people that nothing else can, if it's well done.

AC: Also, you're dealing with painful subjects quite often: sexuality, fidelity in relationships or marriage, identity, family pain.

BG: I'm trying to do that. I'm not saying I'm achieving it, or getting it right.

AC: Humour is also an avenue into those topics, in your work. It's another way of dealing with painful experiences.

BG: But also, what it does, in fiction, is it forces you to look at something differently. That's the other thing you're trying to say. You looked at it this way, now how about looking at it this way instead? No, you don't like that? Okay, put the book down, close it. But I offer this.

AC: Thank you. Would you read the closing section of *The White Bone*?

From *The White Bone*

Mud doesn't tell them about her vision, in which she recognized nobody. She saw, after all, only a small corner of the Safe Place and hardly anyone up close. Neither does she speculate. She nurses her calf, and Bent. She plucks the new grass. She does things delicately, out of contrition and because she is weak with love. At least once an hour she falls into memory and sometimes, coming out of it, she mistakes the smell of Bolt for whomever the memory featured. Bolt is Date Bed, or Hail Stones. Bolt is Tall Time in musth.

Bolt walks under her, She-Snorts in front of her, She-Soothes and Bent follow. Before them are the blue hills, and directly overhead white wads of cloud speed by, going the other way. If you look back, as Mud keeps doing, you can see the dust raised by their passage rolling out as far as the horizon, and the entire plain is washed in light.

Postscript

The interviews collected here were set up to illustrate different national backgrounds within Canadian literature and writers' origins, some of the histories of immigration in Canada and how these writers might perceive them, as well as their responses to national literary traditions, especially the Canadian novel. I was interested in questions of Canadian difference, feminism, writers' careers, responses to colonialism and oppression, and multiculturalism within Canada. I learned a great deal as I went along.

I discovered what I called a politics of "everyday resistance" within Canadian fiction, and social compassion as a strong tradition within Canada, both in terms of immigration and poverty. I also discovered a process of historical and generational change – from Alice Boissoneau's Toronto and Joy Kogawa's Japanese displacement to what Stephen Henighan calls the "dissolution of the nation state in our time," reflected in his own knowledge of and sympathies with Latin America and Easter Europe and Barbara Gowdy's representation of African elephants.

Janice Kulyk Keefer's position on the writing spectrum taught me about Canadian affiliations with minorities within Canada, such as the Acadians, and Maritime regional sympathies expressed in her work. Kogawa's *Obasan* is at the centre of historical and wartime displacement in Canada and a masterpiece in recording that history. Jane Urquhart taught me about some of the Anglo-Canadian or Irish-Canadian responses to the French Empire as well as British Romantic fiction, which she adapts so well in her poetry and novels as she creates new Canadian traditions.

Henighan records his sympathies as being different from those of Americans to Latin America, combining international awareness and Canadian provincialism, an engagement with "all the Americas" and all of their languages.

Globalization seems to have run parallel to urbanization in Canada, reflected in an end to the Western family farm in Van Herk's novel *Judith*, in her genre challenges and in exuberant satire in Gowdy's urban world of Toronto. Gowdy also has a lot of interesting things to say about the conventional family structure inherited from the 1950s and feminism. Van Herk is sensitive to the Canadian north, its peoples and languages, recorded in her award-winning fiction and criticism.

All of the women writers acknowledged the debt they owe to Canadian forebears, sometimes in overturning patriarchal codes and genres, sometimes in implicit influence, literary associations and organizations, and in mentoring friendships.

I wish to record my thanks to all of the writers I interviewed, for their very articulate and finely tuned understanding of Canada and their own writing as they participate in modifying Canadian literary traditions. They were also very sympathetic to multiple histories of immigration and displacement, being rooted in those histories. I hope these conversations will contribute to further conversations about Canadian literature and about the relationships between writers and their world.

Ann Clayton, Guelph, 2017

Biographical Note

Ann Clayton was a teacher of Commonwealth literature at the University of Guelph and the University of Waterloo. She was a teacher of literature at universities in Johannnesburg, South Africa, where she also worked as a writer, free lance journalist and book reviewer.

Her critical articles on literature, arts, culture, and politics have appeared in South African, Canadian and international newspapers and journals. She has published three book-length academic titles: *Olive Schreiner: A Casebook* (McGraw-Hill), *Women and Writing in South Africa: A Critical Anthology* (Heinemann) and *Olive Schreiner* (Twayne). She has also published three previous volumes of poetry: *Leaving Home* (Red Kite / Snailpress), *Eternal Day* (Drum Media) and *Migration* (Vocamus Community Publications).

Since leaving academia, she has worked as a communications consultant for the Federal Government of Canada, working on parliament and policy-making, economic and social justice, women's equality, and international development.

www.ingramcontent.com/pod-product-compliance
Lightning Source LLC
Chambersburg PA
CBHW032047090426
42744CB00004B/114